Crafty Superstar

MAKE CRAFTS ON THE SIDE, EARN **EXTRA** CASH AND **BASICALLY** HAVE IT ALL

By Grace Dobush

NORTH LIGHT BOOKS

Cincinnati, OH
www.mycraftivity.com

13 12 11 10 09   5 4 3 2 1

Distributed in Canada by Fraser Direct
100 Armstrong Avenue
Georgetown, ON, Canada L7G 5S4
Tel: (905) 877-4411

Distributed in the U.K. and Europe by David & Charles
Brunel House, Newton Abbot, Devon, TQ12 4PU, England
Tel: (+44) 1626 323200, Fax: (+44) 1626 323319
Email: postmaster@davidandcharles.co.uk

Distributed in Australia by Capricorn Link
P.O. Box 704, S. Windsor, NSW 2756 Australia
Tel: (02) 4577-3555

Library of Congress Cataloging-in-Publication Data

Dobush, Grace.
   Crafty superstar : make crafts on the side, earn extra cash, and basically have it all / Grace Dobush. -- 1st ed.
      p. cm.
   Includes bibliographical references and index.
   ISBN 978-1-60061-320-3 (pbk. : alk. paper)
   1. Handicraft industries--United States--Management--Handbooks, manuals, etc. 2. Home-based businesses--United States--Management--Handbooks, manuals, etc. 3. Small business--United States--Management--Handbooks, manuals, etc. 4. Success in business--United States--Handbooks, manuals, etc. I. Title.
   HD9999.H363U63 2009
   338.4'77455--dc22

                              2009020378

Editor: Kristin Boys
Designer: Corrie Schaffeld
Production Coordinator: Greg Nock
Illustrators: Rob Warnick, Keith Neltner

www.fwmedia.com

ACKNOWLEDGMENTS

I owe everything to the killer crafters in this book. I'm also sorely indebted to many craft show organizers and the rad folks behind Craft Congress and the Summit of Awesome. (Parenthetical props go out to the ladies of Glitter, who inspired me to get crafty way back in 2000.)

But I owe an especially big thanks to Jessica F. Manack, who represents all that is good in the 412 and was a sounding board for this book from the very beginning.

Major thanks to North Light Books and all its peeps, past and present, and to Pat Jarrett (patjarrett.blogspot.com), a contributor of awesomeness and my go-to photog forever and ever.

Big ups to Brutopia in Cincinnati and Bread N Brew in Wellington, Ohio, for keeping me caffeinated throughout the gestation of this book. And, of course, to my friends and family, who were understanding when I went into hibernation and utterly supportive when I came out of it.

Contents

Introduction

SHOULD I TRY TO SELL THIS STUFF I'M MAKING?

If you're at all crafty, you've probably considered this question. The DIY aesthetic is hot, and why shouldn't you get some of that cash people would otherwise throw at a big box store? Or maybe you'd like to raise awareness and funds for a pet project—whether it's rescuing cats, paying for someone's medical bills or fighting world hunger. Maybe you dream of escaping your cubicle and never going back, or maybe you just want to make a little dough to soften the blow of your credit card bills.

But you have absolutely no clue where to start.

The hundreds of successful crafters who came before you have been there. They feel your pain. They know the uncertainty of traveling a path that's barely been blazed.

That's where this book comes in. I've talked to scores of movers and shakers in the indie craft scene and distilled their vast knowledge into this cute, totable tome. Got questions about tax stuff? You'll get answers. Wonder what your prices should be? No prob. Curious about how crafters get into magazines? I'm on it.

I'm a crafter myself. During my freshman year of college I took a course on book design, which, combined with my background in printmaking, started me crafting, and I never looked back. I put my bookbinding skills to use for friends' wedding albums, then branched out into linocut cards, then started doing blank journals. I joined online craft communities and, inspired by the growing craft commerce scene, cobbled together a Web site. I reached out to established indie crafters for advice—such as Sublime Stitching's Jenny Hart, who I pestered again for this book—and started working the indie craft show circuit.

My business never blew up like Sublime Stitching, but I never really intended it to. My first love's always been writing. And although I absolutely love bookbinding, I can't imagine going full time with it. I prefer to keep my relationship with craft business casual.

And that's why I wrote this book. I wanted a business guide for indie crafters like me who do it themselves and want to stay that way. Whether you're just starting to explore Etsy or are trying to take your biz to the next level, *Crafty Superstar* will help you get where you want to go.

Chapter 1
Do You DIY?

Craft's gotten so popular in the last decade that sometimes it seems like everybody and their grandma are getting on the business bandwagon. And with the dismal economic environment, lots of folks are seeking secondary (or tertiary) sources of income.

This chapter explores the reasons for the handmade craze and explains some of the terms that get tossed around. You'll also figure out what direction your biz should take by meditating on your motivations and expectations. If you just want to cash in on the handmade trend, you may be disappointed. Profits don't come easy, and there's a lot of competition in the DIY marketplace. If you need to make bucketloads of cash to have fun with craft, your heart isn't in it—and buyers will be able to tell. (And this book isn't for you.) But if you really believe in yourself and the things you create, you should go for it. At worst, you lose a few bucks in Etsy listing fees. At best, you get your crafts into the hands of people around the world. Off we go!

WHY HANDMADE?

"The craft world is hotness on top of hotness right now," says Garth Johnson, the man behind the blog Extreme Craft. Aside from the simple satisfaction that comes from making something yourself, there are a couple major reasons for craft's popularity.

People appreciate the personal relationships they have with makers. Lauren Bacon, co-author of *The Boss of You,* says the small scale of craft business is what's important about crafting. "Artisanry is so incredibly valuable now because it keeps us in touch with real human relationships," she says. "When I wear the earrings I bought, I've got a relationship with the person who made them."

Johnson agrees that the rise of crafts stems from a need for community. "I give most of the credit for craft momentum to the organizers behind major craft fairs like Renegade, Art vs. Craft and Felt Club. These are alpha organizers who connected loose groups of people together."

Buying handmade is also a stylish alternative to sweatshops and mass-produced goods. The tagline for Cinnamon Cooper's business, Poise.cc, is, "I'd rather carry a heavy purse than a heavy conscience." She goes to great lengths to make sure all her materials are sweatshop-free. "The interfacing I use is from a company in Germany, and I want all my cottons grown, dyed and printed in the U.S.," Cooper says.

Nobody knows about the rise of the indie craft scene better than Faythe Levine, whose documentary, *Handmade Nation*, and its accompanying book have gotten rave reviews. "The exciting thing about craft and DIY is that everyone can do it," she says. "There's no one saying that you have to do it one way; it's about having the creative urge and following through with it. Deciding what you want to do with it afterward is up to you."

WHAT'S "INDIE"?

Indie, DIY, handmade—there are a lot of different descriptors for the hip things craftsters are creating and selling. You can discuss the semantics for ages, and some people do. (I dare you to ask "what is indie?" at a craft business gathering.) Some people say screen-printed T-shirts aren't handmade enough to be DIY. Others include vintage wares under the indie umbrella. Some exclude items created with mainstream craft kits. Some indie crafts are one-of-a-kind. Some are made entirely from scratch. Some blur the line between fine art and traditional craft. Some blur the line between trash and treasure.

I think of "indie" (stemming from *independent*) as the visual contradiction of combining granny craft techniques with punk sensibilities. A classic example of indie craft (that's been completely co-opted by big-box stores, by the way) is a knit scarf with pink skulls on it.

> **PART OF THE JOY IS THE AWKWARDNESS AND OBTUSENESS OF THE WORD CRAFT. TO SOME PEOPLE, IT MEANS POM-POMS AND PIPE CLEANERS, AND TO OTHERS, A PERFECTLY MADE WOODEN ROCKING CHAIR BY SAM MALOOF.**
>
> **—GARTH JOHNSON**

Indie craft is really similar to indie music in terms of exclusivity—and irony. When it's underground and exclusive, the look has the organic street cred corporate types salivate over. Eventually, the trend catches on with the general public, gets diluted and overdone, and by that point, it's totally over. "One of the last craft fairs that I visited, the Indie Craft Experience in Atlanta, had a bunch of representatives from big companies that flew down to sniff out the newest trends," Johnson says. "I always have an intense love-hate reaction when I walk down the Martha Stewart aisle at Michael's. All of the craft supplies are achingly hip and perfect, but they're being culled and developed by a mega-corporation."

Johnson chooses not to define *craft*. "Part of the joy is the awkwardness and obtuseness of the word. To some people, it means pom-poms and pipe cleaners, and to others, a perfectly made wooden rocking chair by Sam Maloof. At every craft conference, people beat their chests and complain about how craft needs to be defined for everybody to move ahead. I think just the opposite," Johnson says. "*Indie craft* is just as prickly. For some, it's synonymous with 'sloppy craft' and lack of attention to detail. While indie crafters are certainly more cavalier about craftsmanship, I think craftsmanship is becoming more important as crafters get older and gain more experience."

When it comes down to figuring out whether you fit into a scene or under the indie umbrella, the most important thing is to stay true to your ideals and aesthetic. Who says you need a label, anyway?

Garth Johnson on ...
Indie Craft Trends

Crows: The New Sparrows?

"I think about trends in the craft world a lot. After some careful analysis, I think brass knuckles are the new octopi, which were the new owls, which were the new sparrows. Check it out! There are about 200 different brass knuckle–related items on Etsy right now. Sell your stock in octopi and jump on the brass knuckles train."

Disclaimer: Garth made this observation in January 2009. By the time you read this, it's likely that brass knuckles will be totally over and supplanted by ostriches or pocket watches or something.

MOTIVATIONS

Before you decide to cross over from casual crafter to crafty superstar, you should consider two things: your motivations for selling your stuff and your expectations of what will happen when you take your wares to market.

I think the most awesome thing about crafting is the fact that you're your own boss and get to decide what's important to you. Buying and selling handmade gets us further off the grid with each ironic tea cozy and every made-to-order pair of mittens. We know the creation of the product has violated no human rights laws and that its maker was fairly compensated. We can rise above consumer culture and free ourselves from the shackles of big-box stores!

In 2003, Cinnamon Cooper had been making bags for about two years and giving them away to nonprofits for auctions and raffles. She got such glowing feedback and so many requests to buy them that she decided to try to start a business where she'd sell bags and put the profits toward charities she wanted to support but hadn't been able to afford to on her own.

Olivera Bratich's start in the craft business also came through making crafts to raise funds for projects and organizations. "At some point, I looked around and saw a lot of friends who were making really interesting things but had no place in town to sell them," she says. She ended up starting the shop Wholly Craft in Columbus, Ohio. "I started the business with the mission to help people sustain themselves through creative endeavors. These days, I still do some crafting myself—a mix of knitting, papercraft and jewelry making—but most of the time, I'm focused on keeping the shop stocked full of other people's awesome work." And Bratich still holds another job—by day she works in public health, coordinating community planning around HIV/AIDS care.

Hannah Howard started her shop, Lizzie Sweet, because she saw an unfilled need in the beauty market. "I started making perfume because I'm asthmatic. I love things that smell good, but not everything that smells good loves me," she says. "I got into mixing perfume oils, and other people asked for some, too. Lizzie Sweet was born from making and selling things for friends. I like sharing what I do with other people. Making money is not the cake; it's the cherry."

Susie Ghahremani of boygirlparty started her illustrated paper goods business because she liked making things and it was fun to come up with products and new drawings. She says, "Eventually making a living, creating a brand and helping the environment became motivators for me, but not initially. I was just a hyperactive college student when I started."

What Drives Your Craft?

Try this checklist on for size—
check as many motivations as apply.

☐ Making a profit

☐ Making a living

☐ Having fun

☐ Creating a brand

☐ Serving a cause

☐ Helping the environment

☐ Growing your local economy

☐ Other: _____

These are all good reasons to try to take your crafting to the next level. One of them or some of them may apply to you. Or you can make up your own motivation. Whatev! Just be sure your biz matches up with your motivations.

Jesse Breytenbach on ...
Motivations

Jesse Breytenbach is an illustrator and crafter in South Africa who makes beautiful hand-printed fabrics and many other things.

"I think if I only wanted to make money, there are far less complicated ways of doing so. When I discovered craft forums on the Internet, I just wanted to be part of that sharing of ideas. Profit does come into it—I price my goods to make money, partly to keep in line with other crafters and partly because I think it's only worth doing if it is actually profitable. I'd love to make a living doing only what I love, but I'm not ready to give up my day job completely.

"I'm also not sure that I'm the kind of person who can work out what will sell and refine that to come up with a line of products judged purely for profit. Part of my love of crafting is just that—a love. I enjoy making new things, and I particularly enjoy figuring out how to make them. I often take inspiration from my own life, making what I need or want, which is probably not the best business model.

"Helping the environment is a background motivation—I make things on a small scale and pretty much stick to what I can make myself, producing as little waste as possible. I try to use found or vintage fabrics—my initial motivation for block-printing fabric was a 'no waste' one. I didn't want to have silkscreened yardage that I might not use; I thought if I could create a few motifs that I could print in different patterns as I needed them, even cutting out the pieces of fabric for a bag first, and then printing, I'd be able to save fabric."

EXPECTATIONS

After you've chewed on your motivations for a while, it's time to take stock and think about what you'd like your business to look like and if you can really make it happen.

Would I have fun crafting for others instead of myself?

That beaded cochlear coin purse you fussed over for so many hours will go home with someone else after the craft show. Can you bear to never see it again? It's a little like giving away kittens. Rough, dude. If you're accustomed to giving away all your creations for birthdays and holidays, you'll probably be fine. If you've stashed away every amigurumi you ever hooked, you might have a problem.

Would I have fun making similar things over and over?

Unless you specialize in one-offs, you'll likely find a few things that sell like gangbusters and craft to meet the demand. This can mean long nights and a lackluster social life, plus putting your personal projects on the back burner. It could also mean developing a repetitive stress injury. That's why finding joy in crafting is so important. You don't want to lock yourself up like you're in the Triangle Shirtwaist Factory until you perish in the flames of your crafty desire.

Do I have the cash to beef up my output?

Buying more fabric, paper and rickrack might not be so bad, but what if you need a heavy-duty sewing machine, a ginormous printer or an industrial-revolution-size loom? These are things to consider before you bite off more than you can sew. If you're serious about growing your biz, a loan might be something to consider. Or it might mean dipping into savings, reworking your household budget or canceling cable. If you have no pennies to pinch, it's time to get creative in your approach to production. Look into renting equipment or studio time, or reconsider the way you make things. Do you really need virgin wool, or can you use thrift store sweaters?

What makes my product stand out from the crowd?

It doesn't matter whether your main medium is normal knitting or a welding-origami hybrid—another crafter is probably rockin' it, too. But the difference between craft biz and traditional business is that the conflicting interest doesn't necessarily make you mortal enemies. What you're really selling is your personal aesthetic. So your personal style should shine through in everything you make—that's what draws people to handmade stuff. Little details are what can make a product go from being just another mustache-on-a-stick to the must-have novelty of the summer.

Is there an audience for my work?

How many people are in the market for a life-size felted bust of Andrew McCarthy? I mean, really. The great thing about the Internet is that even the wackiest stuff will find a buyer, but there's a certain level of appeal required to be able to sell your stuff with any frequency. If you're OK with serving the small but dedicated group of Brat Pack devotees or just don't feel like going mainstream, that's totally cool.

What do I expect to happen when I put my crafts out in the world?

There are always going to be haters. Can you take the heat? At my first craft show, I made less than $20. Though subsequent shows have been much more successful, I can still count on overhearing someone sniff, "$30 for that?" It can also be overwhelming to encounter crafters whose work is similar to yours—especially if you're selling at the same show. Have confidence in your work and yourself, and you'll be fine.

What makes a crafter successful depends on your definition of success and how you want to achieve it. The three following characteristics will be useful no matter your M.O.: self-confidence, self-motivation and killer organizational skills.

"If you want to be successful, first you must believe in yourself with all your might," plush purveyor Jenny Harada says. "Being doubtful will get you nowhere. Put everything into it that you can. It will be hard work, but it will be yours, all yours, and worth it."

Running a crafty biz means being a Jill of all trades, and you have to be a real self-starter (if you'll pardon the business jargon). The wonderful part of being your own boss is that the biz becomes your baby—you want it to flourish and strive, and I think you'll find that nurturing it comes naturally.

After you've meditated on your motivations and expectations for a little while, you're ready to take your first steps toward becoming a crafty superstar:

1. Pick a name.

2. Google your name to make sure nobody is using it. If somebody else has it, repeat Step 1.

3. Profit!

    OK, so maybe it's not that simple to become a crafty superstar. But it's a place to start.

> IF YOU WANT TO BE SUCCESS-
> FUL, FIRST YOU MUST BELIEVE IN
> YOURSELF WITH ALL YOUR MIGHT.
>
> —JENNY HARADA

Chapter 2
Biz Basics

Since most of us start making crafts purely as a hobby, sometimes it's hard to think about our passion for macramé, lamination or weldigami as a business. (And I'm not even going to start in on the whole left-brain/right-brain thing.) But if you want to be taken seriously—and you do if you wanna get paid—you gotta put down the knitting needles and do some homework.

In this section, we'll go over the deets on naming your crafty business and figuring out what you should charge for your goods. I've got some strategies for boosting production and setting up an optimal workspace, too. And we'll finally get down to the nit-picky details on how to keep your business legal. I'm not a lawyer or a tax adviser, but I'll send you in the right direction to get your business on the up and up.

SETTING UP

If you want people to take you seriously, you've got to consider your business seriously. These simple first steps will get your crafty biz ready to go live.

The name game

When it comes to picking a name, you have to make sure the one you want is actually available. Search on Google and Etsy for businesses and crafters with similar names. For example, you don't want to pick a name like Sublime Stitchery when there's already a Sublime Stitching. It's also worth it to check the database of the U.S. Patent and Trademark Office (www.uspto.gov) to make sure nobody's using the name you want at the national level. And try it out as a dot-com to see if anyone else already has the domain.

It's wise to avoid an overly descriptive name that might hinder you from expanding your business. For example, you wouldn't expect Barbaric Berets to sell anything other than violently French hats. Holly Klump of misshawklet advises, "Never name your business after your username! All your old posts from message boards will come up when people google you."

If you're setting up as a sole proprietorship (which anybody doing business alone automatically is) but are using a descriptive name for your biz, you have to register your fictitious name, sometimes called Doing Business As (DBA) or Operating As (OA). This is done at the local, county or state level—it depends where you live.

> NEVER NAME YOUR BUSINESS AFTER YOUR USERNAME! ALL YOUR OLD POSTS FROM MESSAGE BOARDS WILL COME UP WHEN PEOPLE GOOGLE YOU.
>
> —HOLLY KLUMP

When you pick your name and have ensured that no one else has it, register the Internet domain name, even if you're planning on selling only on Etsy for now. You can set up the URL to redirect to your Etsy store. Through a registrar such as GoDaddy.com, you can get your own dot-com domain for as little as $10.

You've got (to get) mail

Set up a business e-mail address (I'm all about Gmail—the inbox size limits are insane) to keep your biz stuff separated from your personal or work e-mail. Also, since your e-mail address should be easy to find on your Web site, it may result in more spam, and you don't want to junk up your personal e-mail inbox if you don't have to. Consider getting a post office box if you'll be doing a lot of mail orders or if you'd prefer not to put your home as the return address on all your packages. A post office box can cost as little as $10 for a six-month term.

Scope out your business

And now to wrap up some of the last piddling details. You have to nail down the scope of your business. Unless you think a loan application is in your future, you probably don't have to develop a full-blown business plan at this point. Use the questionnaire on the next page to flesh out your business idea and give it life.

You can find an accredited list of dot-com registrars at www.icann.org/en/registrars/accredited-list.html.

Setting Up Shop Questionnaire

What are you going to make and sell?

_____
_____
_____

Where do you want to sell it?

_____
_____
_____

Who's your competition, and what are they up to?

_____
_____
_____

Who are your customers?

_____
_____
_____

How much money do you need to get started?

_____
_____
_____

How much time do you expect to devote to the business?

_____
_____
_____

PRICING

Pricing is a terrifically tricky area. When you're first starting out it's tempting to charge just what you spent on materials, but don't sell yourself short. Charging for the time you spent making each item might make your sticker price seem high, but a person who makes things by hand can't compete with big-box stores' prices. Most people are so far removed from the manufacturing process that they have no idea of what making something really costs.

Customer perceptions

One thing's for sure: If you price your work too low, customers will wonder if it is cheap, and that's no good. In crafting, pricing your work low isn't going to increase demand. Honestly, at an indie craft show you'll see more people buying $5 letterpress cards than flimsy cards that cost 50 cents. Generally, the misers who complain about high prices at shows don't appreciate the hard work it takes to make something by hand. Pay them no mind—they weren't gonna buy from you anyway.

Lauren Bacon, the co-author of *The Boss of You*, a business guide aimed at women, likes to say that handmade goods' high prices aren't high—they're just the real price. "The organic local food industry is a good example of this. Local artisan cheese is so much more expensive than imported cheese," she says. "The cool thing about indie economies is that you get to talk to the people who made it and ask them yourself why it costs what it does. All of those things have real, concrete value."

When you're selling at craft fairs or through Etsy, you can start a dialogue with your customers about pricing and why you charge what you do. "Instead of being afraid, look at the crafters who are established and are charging what they're worth. Ask them how they set their prices, if for no other reason than moral support," Bacon says. "If you're going to a big craft show where a lot of people's prices are lower than yours, practice your answers about why your prices are so high. Have fun with it—make a little FAQ and put it on your table, even. Explain that you use sustainable materials, or that your stitching is time-intensive and impeccable and long-lasting. Engaging with your customers is what gives your product value, because they care about the item, but they also care about their relationship with you."

There are always going to be people whose bottom line is price. They're not your target market, and that's a hard thing for people who love their work to let go. "You'll make compromises and excuses to keep doing what you love," Bacon says. "But look at yourself as an employee and ask, 'Is it reasonable to be paying myself $7 an hour for this?'"

Lauren Bacon on ...
Overcoming Pricing Fear

"A lot of us work from a place of fear that no one's going to pay us what we're worth. When you're running your own business, you should come up with a list of reasons why you are worth that much. Figure out exactly what your costs are, calculate a price and have a friend tell you what they think, because you're probably still undercharging.

"One of the reasons we targeted our book [The Boss of You] at women is that that's something women have a hard time with, saying, 'Sorry, I'm really expensive, and you probably can't afford me.' And I think for men there's a culture where it's cool, and other guys respect you, but other women tend to look at you like, 'Well, you're a little big for your britches,' because women are educated to value modesty really highly."

Setting your prices

Crafters who sell their products go about setting their prices in different ways. For instance, Jessica Manack of Miss Chief Productions has a simple method to price her items. "When I'm creating a product, the first thing I do after I make a prototype is look all over the Internet to see where I can get the materials to make it," she says. "The materials I find partly determine whether I go ahead with making it. I went ahead with the magnet tins I make because of the tins I found." She calculated their price based on how many she could make in an hour.

Samantha Lopez of Knotstudio based her prices on the cost of precious metals and the time-intensive process required to make her jewelry. "I knew coming into this that in the long run it'd be much harder to raise prices than to lower them if they were too high," she says. "I first did a lot of research on the stores that would potentially carry my line and the prices of work they carried. Based on that, I saw that my niche in this case was going to be the rather high-end luxury goods market." Lopez adjusts her prices occasionally, mostly to follow the metal market. "It's important to keep in mind that, although lowering the prices may attract new customers, established clients may feel they were ripped off and take their business elsewhere. Lately, because of the economy, I've decided to keep my smaller silver pieces and offer the larger, more expensive ones only in gold—not only as a luxury but also an investment, as gold tends to hold its value." Her retail prices are simply double the wholesale prices, which is a standard practice.

Calculate the ideal price for your goods using the price calculator in Appendix A (page 122).

Speaking of wholesale, if you even have a single thought of selling wholesale, Bacon advises considering that when setting your retail prices. "Let's say the break-even price you find for your product is $50. When you're a product-based business, you have to think about wholesale price as well as retail. Because there will be a time when some store comes and asks you what your wholesale prices are, and they're going to expect a big discount from your retail price—usually 50 percent. So if you're selling an item for $60 and somebody wants to buy it wholesale for $30, you're losing money."

However you decide to set your prices, it's important to consider all your costs when figuring out your prices as well as how you will sell items (e.g., in sets or individually)—an hourly rate to pay yourself, the cost of materials, administrative stuff, taxes. And don't forget extra things like listing fees, transaction fees and shipping materials and charges.

Let's get down to the nitty gritty of all those extra costs for a minute. Pretend you're selling a card that cost you nothing to make via Etsy for $2. You charge 50 cents for shipping, and you accept payments via PayPal. It's a total profit of $2.50, right? Wrong. Etsy charges 20 cents per listing, plus 3.5 percent of the sale price—that's 27 cents gone. Then, PayPal charges 30 cents per transaction, plus 2.9 percent of the money received—that's another 37 cents. Assuming you already have an envelope, you still gotta buy a stamp, another 44 cents. So your buyer sent you $2.50, but in reality, you've only got $1.42 from the sale. Those little charges are why I sell my linocut cards on Etsy only in packs of six and generally don't list anything for less than $10—otherwise, the fees would eat up all my profit.

FYI

You can easily estimate your postage costs nationally and internationally with the U.S. Postal Service calculator at postcalc.usps.com. If you're shipping from Canada, you can find rates at www.canadapost.ca/Personal/RatesPrices.

BOOSTING PRODUCTION

If you're going big-time, those six-packs of googly eyes and your weekly craft-while-watching-*LOST* schedule probably aren't going to cut the mustard anymore.

Buying all your materials in small quantities from retail craft stores isn't usually a sustainable business plan; doing so will eat up your profits. Search the Internet for your most-used materials—scour Google, eBay, Etsy and other online retailers. You can almost always find better deals when you buy in bulk. This means snapping up enough glass jars, googly eyes and grommets to last you six months instead of just buying what you need whenever you get an order. Buying in bulk will help you keep your expenses and prices down.

And there's no shame in being a scavenger. Hit up every garage sale and Goodwill in the tri-state area for materials. Jenny Harada, who makes kooky stuffed animals, says, "I buy lots of clothes at thrift shops for the sake of repurposing the fabrics. You can get lots of unique material that way!" Keeping an eye on Craigslist (www.craigslist.org) and Freecycle (www.freecycle.org) is also great for finding used goods. Just keep in mind the usual warnings about making Internet transactions—meet in a public place, pay in cash when you have the goods in hand and back out if things seem fishy.

Hannah Howard tries to keep the packaging consistent for her line of Lizzie Sweet body products, but her suppliers sometimes discontinue the jars she uses. "It's hard when you only want to buy a few hundred instead of the huge minimums," she says. So she's had to do a lot of research to find wholesalers who will work with small businesses like hers. "I keep a list of places where I can find things in a bind. It's hard to be consistent with packaging when supply lines are drying up, so I'm focusing on keeping consistent with things that are kind of easy to get."

Julianna Holowka has outsourced some production to keep up with the demand for her Mean Cards. "I was very fortunate to be picked up by two very large retailers recently. For these orders, I shifted production to a local printer," she says. "I chose an independent printer here in Philly with a reputation of being the greenest in the region. Even though those cards are no longer printed by me, I was able to have them printed with soy-based ink and increase the recycled content of my paper—putting out a cleaner product and supporting local business at the same time."

Everything Holly Klump sells on her Web site, www.misshawklet.com, is one-of-a-kind, meaning that what she has on her site is what's for sale. "In a way, it's good because I can keep up," she says. "Then again, if I'm slacking, my shop looks very sad."

It can be tough to stay motivated to produce goods when you're your own boss, you've still got a "real" job and there are no rules. Everybody's different, but you might have some success in setting small goals for yourself. When I'm working on a big project, I like to draw up a calendar that I hang on the wall to write daily or weekly goals on. Or I create routines to get me into the habit of working on my project on a regular basis. For you, this could be taking your knitting projects to your favorite café to work for a whole afternoon every week or setting aside an hour every morning for your crafts. I think it'd be fun to set up a crafting game where, for example, you have to work on your for-profit crafts every time *Law & Order* comes on TV—you'd be a fiend!

> **EVERYTHING SHE SELLS IS ONE-OF-A-KIND. "IN A WAY, IT'S GOOD BECAUSE I CAN KEEP UP. THEN AGAIN, IF I'M SLACKING, MY SHOP LOOKS VERY SAD."**
>
> **—HOLLY KLUMP**

Hannah Howard on ...
Hiring Help

"Once I started getting large orders, I was completely unprepared for it. For a while I told people that I could only make a limited amount of my products, and they could only order up to a certain amount—until I was able to get a part-time worker.

"One thing I wasn't comfortable with was bringing in people who might take what they learned with me to start their own business. It was hard to find people to work with who were just committed to helping. It was also tough to figure out the legalities for paying them and hiring employees. I never wanted to be 'the man.'

"I've hired friends of friends and paid a daily stipend. I never want to create a sweatshop kind of environment. My personal opinion is that you have to pay people at least $10 an hour, and if you pay less, make up for it in food or goodies. I'm a firm believer that you get what you pay for. You also have to be a good judge of character. I only hire people for a short time, like a few days or a night or two, but I've seen other people not be able to pay enough to keep good employees. And if you're looking for people with flexible hours, the pool is small. Luckily, I knew people with odd schedules, like burlesque artists and freelance makeup artists, who could come help me."

FINDING A GOOD WORKSPACE

It's no fun to have to tear down your kitchen table workshop every time you need to eat. This is a good time to finally clean out the attic or take over the guest bedroom. If you're in a small apartment or are otherwise strapped for space, you can always get crafty with it. Think of your setup like a Murphy bed: Create something that you can stash away as is without a lot of fuss. This could be a low table that fits under your bed or boxes of materials that you can pull out of the closet when it's time to get crafty.

Taryn Hipp used to have a dedicated crafting room but now just sets up shop wherever she can. "If I can find a flat surface where there's not a person or an animal, I will fill it with stuff," she says. Hipp runs the online consignment shop My My out of her bedroom. "I have all the My My inventory on this shelving rack that takes up an entire side of my room. The only sign of it being a bedroom is the bed. Otherwise you'd think it was an office. I am completely OCD and love to organize—but I'm also a pack rat. I have a detailed filing system, with a folder for each consigner where I store contracts, invoices, correspondence and payment receipts." The inventory she separates by category and organizes alphabetically.

Holly Klump recently bought a house and turned part of the basement into a studio for herself. "I painted it how I wanted to, and there's no computer down here, so I'm not distracted. I think that's important," she says. "In the last apartment, I had a craft room, but this is like my craft dungeon."

> IF I CAN FIND A FLAT SURFACE WHERE THERE'S NOT A PERSON OR AN ANIMAL, I WILL FILL IT WITH STUFF.
>
> —TARYN HIPP

FYI

Let your insurance company know that you're running a small business out of your home to make any necessary changes to your homeowner's or renter's policy. If you don't have the appropriate riders, the losses to your business might not be covered if a disaster strikes. On the plus side, there are some tax deductions you can claim for a home office. Check with a tax adviser to find out if you qualify for any.

Kati Hanimägi has a well-lit room in her house dedicated to Oddball Press. "It's crammed with my cluttered desk, computer, all my inventory, filing cabinets, a work table, flat files and miscellaneous bookcases," she says. "This is where I design, correspond, pack up orders, store products, and tend to the daily accounting tasks. It's not a picture-perfect organized office—it's full of mismatched bookshelves exploding with stuff, abandoned filing cabinets, an old-school teacher's desk covered with paper trays, a sewing table that the fax machine's on, and three different receptacles to hold recycling." The basement holds her small, tabletop letterpress, but the ceiling is low and there's not a lot of room to work.

If your living space doesn't lend itself to craft production, you might be able to find an artists' co-op or art studio that offers space for a monthly fee or help with maintenance. (See the sidebar on page 36.) Asking around and googling may turn some up in your area. If there isn't anything that fits your needs, DIY!

Holly Klump on ...
Creating a Craft Colony

Six months before she moved away, Holly Klump started a group studio in Burlington, Vermont, called Eight Space. To advertise the space, she posted listings on Craigslist and in coffee shops, and in the small town, word spread.

"I was the most productive when I had that space because it was away from my house. I had set hours when I'd go down there and work. Plus, being around other artistic people is a motivation to work on art stuff. It's also nice to have a public space where you can have shows. It's like an artist colony.

"I was like a landlord, subletting to seven other people. It was kinda cool to be in that leadership position. I started a completely separate checking account for it, which was really helpful. To come up with the price, I determined how many people would fit in the space, estimated the utilities and divided by eight and added a little extra. That extra money helped give the group account a little padding for wine for parties so I never was stuck paying for something that wasn't my responsibility.

"Find someone to help you with legal documents for the sublease agreements, and get a security deposit–that came in handy a couple times. You might have to chase people down for the rent–this is where the padding also helped. Leases were for six months, and if someone had to leave early, we kept the deposit if we couldn't find someone to take over their spot. My biggest piece of advice is to be organized and professional about it. When you're dealing with money and people and their stuff, it can get a little weird."

GETTING PAID
AND KEEPING TRACK

And now for the exciting part—getting paid! Even if you're just starting to make sales, you have to approach your income like a pro. Fortunately, this section covers how to accept payments and keep track of things so the IRS doesn't go after your Hobby Lobby receipts.

If you're going to be staying part-time or small-time, a business loan probably isn't in the cards for you just yet. But you do need a business checking account, especially if you plan on accepting checks from customers made out to your business name. Having an account dedicated to your biz also helps in that, with very little effort, you're creating a record of your business's earnings and expenditures. And don't go nuts when you see those digits rising. "The more money you have saved up to launch your business, the better off you will be," Kati Hanimägi says. "Do not buy anything you do not absolutely need. Be smart. Be thrifty!"

Getting paid through PayPal

PayPal is the gold standard for processing payments online. It's integrated with Etsy and eBay, and many other online retailers use it, too. There are three types of accounts—personal, premier and business. A personal account offers only the most basic services; a premier account allows you to accept credit card payments from buyers. With a business account, you can accept payments from customers via your Web site, via e-mailed invoices or via Virtual Terminal, which works like a credit card swipe machine. Signing up for PayPal is free; the charges come when you receive money from someone. A standard fee is 30 cents per transaction, plus a small percentage. Remember to figure in these costs when setting your prices or shipping charges. (See more about this in the Pricing section on page 27).

If you're using Etsy keep in mind that when you get an order, it's not the same thing as a notification of payment. That comes separately, directly from PayPal. (Make sure your PayPal and Etsy accounts are attached to the same e-mail address—that makes life a lot easier.) If a buyer doesn't send payment within a day or two, send a friendly e-mail letting them know that they still have to pay. Some buyers miss the step unintentionally.

PayPal alternatives

If you're not based in the U.S., you may have to figure out other ways to receive payment, as PayPal doesn't support transactions in some countries. Jesse Breytenbach is a crafter in South Africa who uses Setcom (www.setcom.com), a service similar to PayPal. "It's a bit frustrating, as there are several online marketplaces that I'd love to join, but they aren't set up to deal with anything other than PayPal or checks. Accepting checks in foreign currency incurs such huge fees that it's not worth it for me," she says. "From local buyers, I accept payment simply via direct deposit into my bank account. I prefer not to accept cash; using my bank account means there's a paper trail that makes my accounting much easier."

For accepting credit card payments at craft shows and through your own Web site, ProPay (www.propay.com) is a popular option for crafters. A basic account that lets you process Visa and MasterCard via the Internet is $34.95 a year with small transaction fees and a percentage cut. A premium account, at $59.95 a year, lets you accept Discover and American Express and offers the option to enter transactions by phone.

Bookkeeping

A lot of the crafters I talked to use QuickBooks (quickbooks.intuit.com) for their bookkeeping, and many file their taxes themselves. Holly Klump is a sole proprietor, so her business income is all personal income. "I was able to do everything through TurboTax myself last year. This year I'm budgeting for getting help with taxes," she says. "I like being in complete control of my business. Whatever I do and whatever I put into it is how much I get out of it. It's pretty straightforward that way. If I move, I can move the business with me."

Kati Hanimägi uses QuickBooks for all of her invoicing, banking and credit card ledgers. "I would be lost without it," she says. Taryn Hipp, who also uses QuickBooks, has created spreadsheets in Excel for her specific business needs.

Breytenbach has enlisted the help of a tax consultant ever since an expensive snafu. "One year I forgot to fill in one of the boxes, and the department of revenue asked me for a vast amount of money! I paid it, but then one of my friends recommended their tax consultant. He found the error and got the money back for me. Since then, I've used him," she says. "He receives all my tax documents, makes sure they're filled in correctly and files them for me. I provide him with all my figures, income and expenses. It really helps, knowing that someone else is going to have to make sense of my columns of figures. I keep everything as orderly as I can, to make his job simpler (and faster—he charges by the hour) and so that I can answer any questions he might have easily."

Think you'll need a little help come tax time? Lauren Bacon suggests asking for recommendations from local small business associations. "Word of mouth finds these people best," she says. "Work-at-home bookkeepers can be a good asset—they may be into bartering. And a good bookkeeper will always know a good accountant."

The book *Small Time Operator* by Bernard Kamoroff recommends keeping all tax forms and sales receipts in your files for at least three years.

Lauren Bacon on ...
Accountants vs. Bookkeepers

"A bookkeeper is someone who helps keep your financials up-to-date and your paperwork in order, tracking income and expenses. An accountant is like a lawyer in that they want to know about assets, liabilities, balance sheets, the status of your business—big-picture things. They aren't going to care how much you spent on taking a client out to dinner, but the bookkeeper will pay attention to that. For my business, we didn't get an accountant until we incorporated. Part of that is because we could do our taxes ourselves, and an accountant's hourly rate is often three figures. You could do your books yourself and then go to an accountant to file.

"A bookkeeper can help you set up accounting software, teach you how to use it and chat a few times a year to make sure you're on track. We talk to the bookkeeper when we have a weird expense or an unpaid bill and aren't sure how to record it. We also call on her for random things, like double-checking our payroll calculations and keeping track of the depreciation of our assets. A bookkeeper's a really valuable person to have around."

KEEPING IT LEGAL

If you're going to be all official, there are a few different forms your business can take:

* Sole proprietorship
* Limited partnership
* Limited liability company
* Corporation

Anybody starting a business is automatically a sole proprietor, so that's the business form most of my advice focuses on. When you're a sole proprietor, all the business income is part of your personal income. (And if someone sues your business, they're suing you—the more complicated business forms offer more protection of your personal assets.)

Getting business advice

Now, I'm no legal expert, so please carry out your due diligence with a business adviser, or at least devour some books about running a small business, like *Small Time Operator* by Bernard Kamoroff, which many of the crafter-slash-business-owners I talked to recommended. Check out the offerings for entrepreneurs in your area—local colleges, chambers of commerce or libraries often offer small business classes for free or very cheap.

Holly Klump found a microbusiness development class in her town that got her started. "It was meant for lower-income people trying to start small businesses," she says. "You were hooked up with a business advisor, and it was a nine-month program where they walked you through creating a business plan and helped you figure out your goals." The business plan part was largely focused on people seeking loans for their business—which Klump wasn't—but part of it was about saving money. "My program would double-match you up to a certain amount you saved—if you saved $500, you'd get $1,500. You drew out what you'd spend the money on, and they cut you a check. That's when I registered my business name, had a Web site designed and bought supplies."

Klump found that meeting regularly with her business adviser helped keep her focused and motivated amid many distractions. "I was also finishing my bachelor's degree and working at the time," she says. After registering her business name, she got a tax ID number to be able to write off business expenses and buy wholesale. "Plus, being legal protects you. You can't be making money on the side and not report it," she says. "As much as I'd like to just take my money and run, I think it's better to do things the legal way because you never know what can come back to bite you."

Lauren Bacon agrees. "Always file your taxes and keep receipts. If your goal is to make money and be compensated fairly, you want to track that for your own sake," she says. "If you're a cash-based business, you're on the honor system with the government."

> AS MUCH AS I'D LIKE TO JUST TAKE MY MONEY AND RUN, I THINK IT'S BETTER TO DO THINGS THE LEGAL WAY BECAUSE YOU NEVER KNOW WHAT CAN COME BACK TO BITE YOU.
>
> —HOLLY KLUMP

Getting Legal Advice

If you decide to incorporate your business or need help with contracts or copyright issues, you want the help of a lawyer. Susie Ghahremani of boygirlparty has sought legal assistance for trademark and copyright infringement problems. "Since I'm an artist, I've had to defend and protect my artwork from misuse and imitation," she says. "I've also worked on contract negotiations with lawyers, who understand the terminology of contracts and agreements better than I ever will."

Bacon recommends looking for someone who's a litigating lawyer. "Some lawyers never go near the court," she says. "If you've got a great style and need to watch for people infringing on it, it's a real benefit to you to have a litigating copyright lawyer on your side. You have to find someone who's a bit of a shark."

Not sure where to find a lawyer? Bacon suggests three routes:

- Ask other crafters who they work with. "Go to networking events for crafters and anyone who's in a similar kind of business," she says. "You have to find someone you can trust, who can protect you, who's smart and understands a little about your industry and what you want. If they're used to dealing with megacorps, they're not even going to understand the concept of your biz."

- Contact professional associations for lawyers. "The staff can give recommendations of people to call," she says. "It's going to be different depending on what you need— incorporating and intellectual property/copyright issues might require two different lawyers. Or it might not."

- Ask your hairdresser. "They might not know the best lawyer, but they'll know the best gossip about them."

When you find some possible BLFs (best lawyer forever), do your homework before your first meeting: read up on the legalities of what you're doing so you can ask good questions. "Meet with a few people and ask them pointed questions about the stuff you've learned, with concrete examples from your business," Bacon advises. "That'll test their knowledge and gauge how respectful they are with you. Lawyers have a crazy high hourly rate, so you want to know you're getting your money's worth."

A lawyer's job is to help you assess legal risks and watch out for pitfalls. If they're worth their salt, they'll ask you lots of questions about your business and where you're going. Ask about their background, who their other clients are and what their primary areas of expertise are. Then describe the kind of legal advice you need, and ask explicitly if those are services they provide. If you're on the fence, ask for references. "I do that all the time. If I'm moving into a building, I ask to talk to another tenant and ask them about the landlord," Bacon says.

"An ideal situation for an indie crafter is to find a lawyer who will give a discounted rate in return for some other concession, such as correspondence via e-mail rather than meeting in person, with a turnaround time of a few days for responses," she says. "Ask the lawyer straight up: 'What's the most effective use of the time I pay you for?' The nice thing about lawyers is that they work insanely efficiently. So gather together all your queries at once. Lawyers teach us a valuable lesson about efficiency. I'll be like, 'We have 13 agenda items and 15 minutes to get through them all. Let's go!'"

Generally, lawyers will give you itemized invoices if they're on a monthly retainer; you'll pay for things such as couriers, long-distance charges and travel costs—all of which is spelled out in the contract you and the lawyer agree on at the beginning of your relationship. If you don't have the lawyer on retainer, you'll just get a bill upon completion of the project.

FYI

For a list of legal and other small business resources, check out Appendix E on page 138.

Jenny Hart on ...
Dealing with Copycats

The Sublime Stitcher herself has dealt with some nasty knockoffs of her work. Generally, she recommends going straight to a lawyer when dealing with a corporate copycat and trying to resolve things crafter-to-crafter when it's a solo scofflaw.

"It's a very difficult situation to navigate. If a person feels that copyright infringement is going to be an issue for their business, I think it's a good idea to consult with a lawyer to see what steps should be taken in structuring your business (such as establishing copyrights, trademarks or patents), what type of language you may want to use to communicate your copyrights and how to pre-frame potential infringements.

"But, I also think it's wise to understand that most lawyers will look at any situation along the lines of worst case scenario and will lay out every possible action—which can be really scary to consider. But that's their job, and it's their responsibility to look at it that way. It's ultimately up to you to decide the best and most effective course of action."

Chapter 3
Selling Out

So you've figured out how much your plastic-canvas cupcakes are going to cost and found the perfect URL. But how are you going to get them into the hot little hands of the adoring public? You've got a lot of options.

The Internet helped fuel the indie craft revolution, so it's no surprise that so many handmade goods trade hands online. Selling through a site such as Etsy or through your own online storefront is a great entry point into craft commerce. But there are still IRL options. I'll show you how to get started placing your goods into bricks-and-mortar shops on consignment or wholesale.

Whatever your sales strategy, you'll make good use of the tips on taking great photos, polishing your packaging and dealing with customers. Get ready to sell out!

WHERE TO SELL

One of the most awesome things about DIY business is the number of distribution options you have. No matter what you sell, how much you can produce or how good (or bad) you are with the Internet, you'll find an option that fits your needs.

Your own Web site

How it works: You build a Web site where people can buy stuff.

Costs involved: Quite a few, including domain registration, hosting fees, online payment processing fees and a Web designer if you aren't HTML-literate.

Pluses: You are the master of your domain. The possibilities are endless!

Minuses: The initial setup costs a lot more than going with Etsy. It might be a headache if you want to be a crafter, not a webmaster. Plus, you have to let people know the site even exists.

Advice: If you're into DIY Web design or have a roommate who dreams in XHTML, go for it! Do link trades with other crafters and follow the promotion tips listed in Chapter 5. (For more on setting up a Web site, see page 56.)

Online consignment shops

How it works: You send in your stuff to the store organizers, set your prices and leave the selling up to them.

Costs involved: A portion of your selling price, plus shipping fees and your trust.

Pluses: It doesn't require a lot of maintenance and circumvents the traditional retail system.

Minuses: Because it's not exactly easy or lucrative to keep track of hundreds of $2 items, organizers sometimes flake out. There's also no guarantee that your items will sell.

Advice: Stick to established shops, or at least go with ones recommended by friends. Check out the list of shops on page 141.

Etsy

How it works: You create an online storefront for your brand and sell as many or as few of your crafts as you like.

Costs involved: Small listing fees and sales fees apply for every transaction. You also should consider the cost of shipping, though you can pass that on to the consumer.

Pluses: Thousands of shoppers browsing the site constantly, and it's a breeding ground for blog fodder.

Minuses: Tens of thousands of items are for sale on Etsy, so it can be tough to stand out.

Advice: Having awesome pics is the first step to making a killing on Etsy. It's possible to pay extra to be a featured crafter. Get familiar with other crafters on the site, and star items and sellers that you like. Getting a mention on a major craft blog (see the appendix on page 134 for names) is a surefire way to sell out your store.

Etsy listings are active for three months. As time goes on, your listings move toward the end of the site's search results. When you renew your listings, you get back to the first page of results. So renew often!

Setting up Shop on Etsy

The anatomy of an Etsy storefront is pretty simple, but there are lots of little details to pay attention to. Here's the Etsy shop of Miss Chief Productions (misschief.etsy.com) as an example.

1 **Store banner:** An eye-catching banner that reflects your brand is important. It doesn't have to be complicated; in fact, less is often more. Follow the exact specifications for the image size you upload—you don't want the pic to be squished or stretched!

2 **Shop announcement:** Use this space to welcome visitors. Also make note of upcoming shows you're doing, if you're going to be unable to ship orders for a short time, recent press mentions and any other news.

3 **Featured listings:** Pick out three new or especially awesome items in your shop to give them top billing.

4 **Sections:** Creating sections lets shoppers browse by item type within your store. You can create up to 10 different sections under the Your Etsy>Shop Setup area.

5 **Item listings:** Make sure your individual listing titles are descriptive, but not so long that they get cut off.

Craft shows

How it works: You pay for table space and sell your brains out.

Costs involved: You pay an application and/or table fee, plus any travel costs and possibly a vendor's license and sales taxes.

Pluses: Selling at a show is great exposure, and it's an exciting atmosphere where you can meet buyers and other crafters.

Minuses: There's no guarantee of sales—or good weather. You also have to be prepared to be on your feet all day. Competition can be tough to get into big shows.

Advice: Do it if you can afford to get to the venue. Go in with a friend if you're hesitant or want to split the expenses. See the next chapter for more advice on indie craft shows.

Bricks-and-mortar stores

How it works: Many small shops buy work from individual artisans wholesale. You set your price—generally half of your retail price—and a store buys stuff from you to resell. Or they might host your work on a consignment basis, meaning they display and sell your work in exchange for keeping a percentage of the retail price.

Costs involved: Aside from the deep discount you have to offer, dealing with established stores will absolutely require you to stay straight with the IRS. You might also need to supply a retail display.

Pluses: The general public sees your stuff, and the shop's interest is a real endorsement for your work.

Minuses: You'll bring in less cash than if you sold items yourself. Also, you rely on the store's reputation, and it's worth keeping in mind that many stores don't survive past their first year.

Advice: Scope out boutiques in your area and ask if they sell local designers' work. If it seems like a good match, arrange a short meeting to present your work, or give them your URL. Find out whether they prefer to buy wholesale or on consignment. It might be easier to get your work into a consignment-based store, since the risk for the shop is relatively low. If you're planning on pursuing wholesale, develop a price list to have on hand.

Kati Hanimägi on ...
Selling Wholesale

Kati Hanimägi runs Oddball Press in Cleveland, Ohio.

"I began by creating a mailing list of about 500 specialty retailers—mostly stationery and gift stores. I created the list by researching different cities online, searching through shopping guides. If I felt the store might carry similar products, I added them to my list. I also asked friends and family for names of shops in their areas. Then I sent out my first catalog, introducing our line of 18 greeting cards. I sent card samples to 100 stores I thought had the most promise. I had the Web site up and ready, and basically crossed my fingers, hoping someone would order. I made the uncomfortable follow-up calls that everyone says you need to do, but I never got any orders from the cold phone calls. Since that first mailing, I've continued to send direct mail pieces that showcase new products. I'd recommend it to any crafter looking to break into the wholesale market.

"My biggest move to generate business in the wholesale market was to attend the National Stationery Show. It was a fantastic way to meet retailers, reps and fellow crafters. Our sales doubled, and we met many people. But it was a large expense between the booth, travel, being in New York City and other odds and ends. If you do a trade show, create a budget, stick to that budget, and come up with conservative sales projections."

Olivera Bratich on ...
Approaching Shops

Olivera Bratich opened crafty supermarket Wholly Craft in Columbus, Ohio in 2005.

"Before approaching us, do a little homework. If you can, visit the shop in person to see if your items would be a good fit and if we carry anything similar already. If you're not in the area, read all the information offered on the Web site and check out other crafters we work with. This will give you a good idea of the context your work will be displayed and sold in, and how best to approach the shop.

"Approach a shop with a selection of your popular designs and pieces, not the stack of unsold items you have leftover from a craft fair. We have to make a decision on your entire line, so show your best work. If you're submitting work online for consignment consideration, invest a little time in learning to take good photos. And never get discouraged by rejection from any shop. Often it's not a direct reflection of your work. The shop may not be a good fit for your style or they might already carry something similar. In our case, our space is pretty limited, so at times we're not taking any new items in a particular category until we clear out what we have to make space."

Olivera Bratich stocks Wholly Craft with handmade paper goods, clothing, home decor, jewelry and more.

GET A WEB SITE

Even if you're planning on selling your wares exclusively through Etsy, wholesale orders or at craft shows, a Web site can be one of the most valuable tools a crafter has for generating sales. Nobody will buy your decoupage candy bean earrings if they don't know you exist and have no way of finding you. Plus, it's helpful for people to know a little bit about you and your business before they commit to a purchase.

You don't need to be a Web-design genius to get a site set up. One easy option is to register a free blog and redirect your own URL to it. (For more on blogging, see page 98.) You can do this by logging into the site where you registered your URL and creating a forward or redirect. You can integrate your Etsy and Flickr accounts with a blog very easily, and blog updates are a snap.

You can also try enlisting the help of an HTML-gifted pal to create a Web site. See if she's interested in exchanging services—say, she builds you a Web site, you give her 30 plush octopi. It's a match made in heaven. Cinnamon Cooper of Poise.cc found a friend willing to do her Web site for free if she gave him free rein. (You can see the stunning results on the opposite page.) "Even if you don't know a Web designer, look for a college student trying to build their portfolio," she suggests. "They'll ask questions you never considered—stuff like, 'What color is your business?' You learn how to explain and describe the feel of your business to someone who's creative but unconnected to it."

> THE DESIGNER WILL ASK QUESTIONS YOU NEVER CONSIDERED-STUFF LIKE, 'WHAT COLOR IS YOUR BUSINESS?' YOU LEARN HOW TO EXPLAIN AND DESCRIBE THE FEEL OF YOUR BUSINESS.
>
> —CINNAMON COOPER

Your Web site should show what you and your products are all about. Poise.cc's super-stylin' homepage flaunts Cinnamon Cooper's ethics as well as her wares. Bold links lead visitors further into the site, and there are no questions about Cooper's prices or policies.

Or you can DIY! "I'm a big nerd and I made the My My Web site myself. As far as DIY goes, HTML is an awesome thing to know," Taryn Hipp says. "When you have your own Web site, you have full control of it—you can promote it the way you want and to whom you want."

Regardless of which direction you go, your Web site absolutely must include these things:

- **Pictures of your crafts.** Even if you're not selling directly from your Web site, post lots of high-quality pictures (see the sidebar on page 60) and detailed descriptions. Organize your products by category, kind or theme so they're easy to browse.
- **Information about yourself.** Knowing something about the maker is what makes buying handmade so awesome. You don't need to share your entire life story or your full name; background information on how you started crafting, what you make and what inspires you will suffice.

- **Ordering policies.** For example, include where you sell your wares, how you accept payment, how quickly you ship and whether you accept returns. If you find people asking the same questions over and over, that's a good cue to add it to your FAQ.
- **How to contact you.** Include an e-mail address, a contact form and/or a business phone number. If you have a business mailing address or P.O. box, include that, but don't post your home address.

On a similar subject, your Web site must not under any circumstances contain:

- Eye-bleeding color combos
- Seizure-triggering flash graphics
- Slow-loading giganto photos instead of thumbnails (the Save for Web option in Photoshop should be your BFF)
- Blurry or washed-out photos
- Images of things you didn't make
- Text in cRaZy uPpEr-LoWeR-cAsE type

Susie Ghahremani's illustration style comes through on boygirlparty. com. The left column highlights her latest product, and the straightforward links make it easy for shoppers to find what they're looking for.

How to Make Your Own Light Box

Make your own light box to help you get those picture perfect merchandise photos. All you need is a large sheet of white drawing paper, a stack of books and three desk lamps to get really professional-looking photos. (Note: this works best on smaller items.)

1. Make a stack of heavy books, about a foot high, on a table or desk. Get three desk lamps with bendy necks; use daylight or full-spectrum light bulbs to avoid giving your whites a yellow cast.

2. Put one end of the sheet of paper over the top of the stack of books; it should be big enough to cascade in front of the books and onto the desk, forming a mini stage. Don't crease or bend it—the paper will be your seamless background.

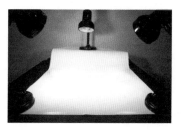

3. Put one lamp on top of the book stack to hold the paper in place and point the head toward the "stage" area. Place the other two lamps on the left and right sides of the stage area. Each bulb should be about a foot away from the object you're photographing; adjust the distances if necessary.

Now you're ready for your close up!

Picture Perfect

The photos you post online are the first impression you make, so you've got to take the best pictures you can. (And featured sellers on Etsy always have really sweet photos.) The following photo tips are crafter-tested and author-approved.

1. **Invest in a digital camera.** You don't have to spend a fortune to get a quality camera—you can find one for less than $150 that does everything you need it to do. (I've been using Canon PowerShots for five years.) Make sure it has macro settings for detail shots, and spring for the extra-large memory card.

2. **Make 'em big.** Set the resolution high—300 dpi and at least 1200 × 1600 pixels. You'll resize them for the Web, but you need high-res images on hand in case Super Glossy Magazine comes calling.

3. **Set the scene.** Busy backgrounds are major buzzkills. Never take pictures of your wares against your bedspread or, even worse, your rec room's shag carpet. Plain backgrounds put all the focus where it should be: on your products.

4. **Light it up.** Natural light is always best, but using a light box is even better for capturing details. (See page 59 to learn how to make a DIY light box.). Never use a built-in flash for close-ups. It will wash out your image beyond recognition.

To show off her stenciled tea towels, Jesse Breytenbach shot them in a staged setting using natural light.

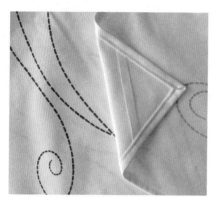

A close-up shot—like this one of Breytenbach's tea towels—shows off details that make your product stand out as well as show off your craftsmanship.

5. Take four. Design*Sponge's Grace Bonney recommends crafters get four pictures of every item: a close-up shot, a full shot, a situation shot and a shot that shows how your product is unique, like that Bolivian chain stitch your nana taught you. Use the macro setting on your camera to get the close-ups; if you're within 8" (21cm) of the product, it's the only way to keep the image crisp.

6. Polish up. You don't need Photoshop to make your photos awesome—there are plenty of cheap or free options out there, such as Photoshop Effects, the open source GIMP and the online Picnik (which is integrated with Flickr). If you lack mad Photoshop skills, just use the AutoCorrect color and brightness/contrast features to fix up your photos. Skip the sharpness options, though. If your original image is fuzzy, artificially sharpening it will look wack.

7. Save it all. Create a naming system that makes it easy to figure out exactly which pictures are which. Use something like 2009-redteacozy-300dpi.jpg instead of the default DSC01028.jpg. Back up your photos periodically by burning them onto CDs, saving them on an external hard drive or uploading them to an online storage system. It seems like a hassle—but only until it's coulda-woulda-shoulda time.

PRESENTATION

It's all about first impressions. If you mail off your handmade soap in a sandwich bag filled with glitter, all you're going to do is tick off your customers (and possibly cause major skin irritation). When you start selling, you have to create a consistent look for your crafts.

When it comes to packaging, you might only need something as simple as a tag for your soft goods, or you might need a sturdy sheath that can double as a mailer. Where you're selling also determines to some extent the wrapping you require. A simple wrapper might suffice for an Etsy sale, but if you want to sell wholesale to boutiques, you need something that's eye-catching and can stand on its own.

I love packaging that's elegant and simple. Your package could be as simple as using a custom-printed wide rubber band to hold together a stack of hand-printed cards. The main thing is to create a look for your crafts' packaging that accurately represents your style and motivations. (You can find great examples of packaging at www.flickr.com/groups/etsypackaging.) When you come up with a look you like, invest in bulk orders of bags, mailers, stickers and other supplies from eBay or wholesale retailers to keep your per-item cost low.

Remember that packaging also has to protect your goods, not just look pretty. Jenny Harada, who makes plush creatures, uses the free priority boxes from the post office. "I put all my items in plastic zip bags in case the package gets wet," she says. "I bought a bunch of large zip bags from a wholesale supply place. It's so worth it to keep the goods intact and bundled together so they don't fall out all over the place when the box is opened."

When you ship off an order, add a personal message that lets the customer know you appreciate their business and reminds them there's a real person behind the product. I like to write a little thank-you note on a cool piece of vintage paper.

Holly Klump's tags for her yarn are simple and to the point—tied on with yarn (of course!) with the logo in a loopy font.

Jesse Breytenbach's brooches are wrapped in a scored kraft tag, which is stamped and fastened with ribbon.

Mix-and-Match
Packaging Concept Worksheet

DIRECTIONS: Make a copy of these pages. Cut out the boxes along the dotted lines and place the slips of paper into one of three containers: one for the basic package, one for modifers and one for padding. Then the fun begins! Choose one (or two) boxes from each container to come up with a packaging concept. Or you can just look at the list and choose the ones you like best. Whatever.

BASIC PACKAGE

cardboard box

scored fold-over mailer

shoebox

poly bag

envelope

takeout box

cloth or mesh bag

poster tube

lunch bag

glass jar

paper grocery bag

static-proof bag

gift box

glassine paper envelope

butcher paper

paper coffee cup

MODIFIERS

screen printing

personalized stickers

spraypainted stencils

stapled labels

collaged cutouts

decorative tape

colored vinyl or duct tape

string

stitching

wide rubber band

stamps

PADDING

tissue paper

shredded junk mail

fabric scraps

bubble wrap

newsprint

foam sheets

vintage sewing patterns

kraft paper

fake grass

CUSTOMER SERVICE

The orders are rolling in! How do the crafty superstars keep track of it all?

Some crafters keep Excel databases of all their orders; others put the info on index cards and attach them to baskets to fill with the orders. No matter your system, keeping your workspace in order will help you fulfill orders quickly. (You can use the forms in the appendix on pages 128-129 to help keep track of your orders.)

"I have a very small business, so my inventory is in labeled plastic bins," says Holly Klump. "As far as orders go, I fill them every night when I get home from work. I mainly keep track of them through Etsy and PayPal, which is what I use to take orders."

Susie Ghahremani goes the Excel route. "As a sole proprietor, I don't need anything fancy, just a database and a well-labeled filing system for papers and receipts," she says.

If any issues arise between when the buyer places an order and receives it, communicate with them any issues promptly and plainly. Be straightforward—no excuses. State on your Web site or in your Etsy shop what days you normally ship items and how long order fulfillment will take.

"In the best of bad situations, a talk can help clear up giant misunderstandings," Ghahremani says. "One of the perks of being a small, crafty business is that pretty much everyone you work with has a name, a face, a personality, and is real, unlike faceless gigantic corporations. So talking things out is a very real solution to problems."

Faythe Levine tries to answer all e-mails within a day. "If I get an e-mail and I don't respond right away, I know it's gonna be at least a week until I get back to it," she says.

Crafters love to share information and experiences, but what if someone's getting a little too nosy? When people ask Hannah Howard of Lizzie Sweet how she makes her bath and beauty products, she jokes, "I'd tell you, but I'd have to kill you. I'm like, 'Dude, there's a price tag on it. I'd tell you, but not without you paying me something for it.'" Humor is the great deflector.

Customer service scenario guide

Every crafter is bound to run into a problem sooner or later. Learn how to deal with some common issues with this scenario guide with commentary from Jessica Manack of Miss Chief Productions.

Scenario #1
A customer says they paid, but you never got the money.

What to do: First off, confirm all the information—did the customer send the payment to the right address or the correct PayPal account? Ask for a proof of payment. Manack advises that you state on your Web site that items ship upon receipt of payment or check clearance. "Clearly lay out which kinds of payment you prefer. PayPal is a really safe way of accepting payments—money orders and cash can just get taken from the mail. If someone sends a check, send them a confirmation e-mail to let them know when you get it," she says. "When I get an order, I let the customer know when I'll ship the order and via which service." Being overly communicative is a good way to prevent customers from getting frustrated. And never send out an order without getting the cash in hand. You'll find it's a lot harder to track down payments after the customer's already got the items.

Lesson learned: Using an online payment system like PayPal takes the responsibility of payment processing off your hands.

Scenario #2
The customer never received an order.

What to do: Check all your records to be absolutely sure you sent the package to the correct address and also make sure that it isn't crammed in your messenger bag or under the seat of your car. My policy is to respond right away, telling the customer what date I sent the package, via which shipping service and apologize for the delay. Ask the customer to let you know if the merchandise hasn't arrived in a week, and follow up if he or she doesn't get back to you.

Sometimes the mail is just delayed and the problem resolves itself, but sometimes your package disappears into some crafty Bermuda Triangle. If this is the case, I usually offer to send a replacement at my own cost and ask the buyer to return one item if both eventually show up. If the item was one-of-a-kind, offer a replacement or store credit. Manack suggests working delivery confirmation into your shipping fees if your products are pricey. You can also state in your shop that you offer delivery confirmation and insurance, but at an added cost. If you're shipping internationally, things can get caught up in customs, causing delays. Within the U.S., you can verify addresses at www.usps.com. Manack always gets the ZIP+4 for addresses. "I've heard that if you add that, it makes your shipping faster, and it's also a way to double-check the address," she says. It doesn't hurt to compare an Etsy address with the PayPal address, too.

Lesson learned: Consider springing for delivery confirmation and insurance, and always double-check mailing addresses.

Scenario #3
A hater starts bad-mouthing your biz online.

What to do: Anybody who's reached a moderate level of success has encountered somebody like this. Maybe bittergirl89 is leaving nasty feedback or is trolling around your favorite message board with mean-spirited responses to you. Generally, there's not a lot to be done in regard to haters, aside from ignoring them.

"Don't get caught up in it," Manack says. "Correct misinformation politely, and feedback helps keep people in line. Feedback helps customers make good decisions, and it makes you seem more transparent." If the person crosses the line of defaming your business and tarnishing your character, it might be worth it to trace the person's IP address and contact the Internet service provider to let them know about their customer's breach of service.

Lesson learned: Rise above the hate.

Scenario #4
You've received a large order from Nigeria.

What to do: It seems unlikely, but even artists and crafters are targets for e-mail scams. Often the e-mail expressing interest in your wares will be vague, without mentioning specific items. Sometimes the person purports to be a shop owner who'd like to carry your wares. Other times the person says he's traveling and needs you to ship to an intermediary, and he offers to cut you a check for a lot more cash for the inconvenience. The bottom line: Never accept overpayments or give out your bank account information, and avoid using wire services for any transaction. If you think the customer is legit, wait to ship your goods until you have the money in your hand—international transfers or money orders can take a week or two to clear.

Lesson learned: If it sounds too good to be true, it probably is.

Scenario #5
Somebody is selling a blatant copy of one of your crafts.

What to do: First, take a breath and get some perspective. Ask a friend if you're overreacting before you take your case to Judge Judy. It might only take a conversation with your competitor to straighten things out. But if you can't reach an acceptable resolution, consider taking legal action. This kind of scenario is a good argument for filing copyrights. What if the perpetrator isn't some punk with an Etsy shop but rather a corporation that copped your style? A terse e-mail isn't likely to do much. Find a lawyer who specializes in intellectual property and copyright.

Lesson learned: Consider copyrighting your work.

HOW TO NOT SELL

The awesome thing about being in an alternative economy like crafting is that you can set your own rules. Maybe you're OK with just breaking even, perhaps you want to use your business to support charitable causes, or maybe you just want to create stuff to trade with other artisans.

Trades are a long-standing tradition in the creative communities. I love doing them—after my hairstylist found out I was a bookbinder, we did an exchange: I made her a journal to her specifications, and she gave me a haircut. Score! I first got in touch with crafter Jesse Breytenbach through a printed fabric swap. Crafty message boards often will have an area devoted to trades, which is a really fun way to make use of pieces you don't intend to sell.

Lauren Bacon, co-author of *The Boss of You*, has a very fashionable trade agreement between her Web design company and a local clothing designer. "We update her site every spring and fall with her new collections," Bacon says. "We track our time and then go to her store and get the amount of clothes that corresponds with the value of the time we spent working on her site." But Bacon also warns that you shouldn't trade with just anybody. If you don't really need $200 worth of bedazzled eye masks, just say no! "If you weren't intending to be a charity, it can be not very fun," she says.

Cinnamon Cooper started Poise.cc giving half the cost of her bags to women-focused charities, but she realized that with the costs of running a business and buying fabric, she was losing money. "It was fine at first, but after I got to the point where I wanted to make it sustainable, I realized that making enough money to pay off my credit card purchases would be a good thing," she says. Now, just select bags are associated with nonprofits, with about 20 percent of her sales going to charity. If you donate your goods to a registered nonprofit, get receipts so you can use the deduction on your taxes.

Hannah Howard on ...
Bartering

"The guy who drew the Lizzie Sweet girl [below] did it for a scarf. I rely on contracts—if I'm going to do something for someone, I make sure I have it in writing and that we agree on the terms. It just keeps everybody in the clear. Contracts can make people nervous sometimes, but it's not that the other person doesn't think you're honest, it just gets you on the same page. I got a contract template off the Internet and altered it for my barters. Sometimes an e-mail conversation with the details is enough, but if it's not in writing, it can be kind of mercurial."

Chapter 4
Indie Craft Shows

The first thing "craft show" conjures up in most people's minds is a junior high-gymnasium affair with vendors hawking starched doilies, garish tole paintings and lawn geese attire. My own first venture into craft commerce was at a show in a church basement. The table fee was less than $20—but so was my total revenue for the day.

Thankfully, the indie craft show came along. In the last decade, the number of shows catering to alternative crafts has exploded, so the unorthodox crafter has boundless opportunities, from a couple card tables set up in a café to truckzilla-size shows. Sales can be good or bad, but every show is still a promotional opportunity. If there aren't any indie craft shows in your area, consider starting one of your own! It takes some work, but you can do it on the cheap and help cultivate a craft community in your own town.

Quiz: What Kind of Crafter Are You?

You don't need to be the next Jenny Hart to clean up at a craft show, but you should have your little ceramic pirate ducks in a row. The results of this quiz will give you tailored suggestions for taking on the indie craft show circuit.

1. Are you already selling your stuff online or in shops?

a. Here's my URL and my publicist's number.

b. I've been thinking about it.

c. Why would I? My grandma buys me out before anyone else can.

d. Yeah, on Etsy!

2. Does your business have a name?

a. yes, and a trademarked logo and a spin-off brand for kids

b. not really

c. Kat's Kountry Krafts

d. I just came up with one: Glittercraft Flutterbuy!

3. Have you spent much time developing and perfecting your crafts?

a. Well, yeah—otherwise I wouldn't have gotten that shoutout in *BUST*.

b. I feel most secure when covered in glue.

c. I've got toilet paper cozies down to a science.

d. I do most of my crafting at my weekly Stitch 'n Bitch.

4. How would you describe your style/aesthetic?

a. sleek, chic and cheeky

b. quirky, dark and entirely indie

c. potholders only my grandma could love

d. sparkly, fluffy and fun!

5. What words would you use to describe yourself?

a. confident, outgoing, ambitious

b. shy, moody, introverted

c. traditional, cautious, kitschy

d. friendly, optimistic, happy-go-lucky

6. Have you ever been to a craft show?

a. I hit up Renegade and Bazaar Bizarre every year.

b. I prefer not to go outside.

c. I hit up every craft show/bake sale in the tri-county area.

d. I sell at a local indie trunk show.

7. How do you feel about crunching numbers in your head?

a. No problem—I was a mathlete.

b. I am incapable of making change.

c. Why do I need to crunch them?

d. That's what calculators are for.

8. Do you like interacting with the public?

a. I know how to rope them in and make the sale.

b. I told you before—I prefer not to go outside.

c. I love trading plastic canvas tips.

d. I am all about meeting other crafters.

9. What's your ideal craft show location?

a. anywhere I can go with my frequent flier miles

b. my own apartment

c. a church basement or high school gym

d. anything within driving distance

10. What do you want to get out of your craft show experience?

a. achieve total craft domination

b. not have any panic attacks ... and sell some stuff.

c. connect with other proponents of traditional macramé.

d. meet other crafters, make some money and have fun!

Turn the page to find out your quiz results!

Quiz Results

How'd you score?

Mostly A: Biz Maven

Your mad craft skills are paralleled only by your ability to juggle invoices, inventory and iChat while blogging about your latest batch of vendibles. But for as much as you've got it going on in the business department, you could use some extra pointers on how to really flex your craft connections. Pay special attention to the advice in this chapter on etiquette. And if your town doesn't have a show, check out the section on starting your own, you overachiever.

Mostly B: Craft Hermit

No crafter is an island. You are a whiz with a Dremel, but when your only social outlet is Craftster, isolation is likely to dull the shine on your sequins. Make a day trip to scope out the nearest craft show, bring your Paxil and a pen, and I promise you'll be inspired—you might even make a few friends. Read up on customer service and craft show etiquette, and you'll be ready to sell!

Mostly C: Old-School Crafter

I'm going to be honest with you—indie craft show organizers are very discerning. It might sound a little elitist, but if you don't fit the aesthetic of a DIY show, you aren't going to get accepted. Irony is totally welcome, but all signs are pointing toward you being really serious about those plastic canvas bookmarks. Check out the scene at your closest indie craft show before you apply to sell at one.

Mostly D: DIY Butterfly

You are all about collaborating with other crafters and don't shy away from your potentially adoring public. Your enthusiasm will go far in making sure you have a good time at a craft show, but you gotta check yourself before you wreck yourself. Don't promise more than you can deliver, and pay extra attention to the business side of things before your first show. Consider sharing a table with a friend!

ARE YOU READY?

Whether she's an old hand dipping or her toes in the craft show kiddie pool for the first time, every crafter has to pick her battles. There are just so many good shows these days that it'd be impossible to hit up every one of them without a legion of employees.

First, check your quiz results on the previous page to determine your crafty fortitude. Consider these things before you start applying to every show that looks cool: your prior craft show experience, how much stock you'd have by the show date and, most importantly, whether you can afford it. The monster shows can cost upwards of $100 a day to display, but small, local shows are often very affordable. Do some rough calculations with the craft show profitability worksheet on page 81 to get an idea of whether you'd break even at a show you have to travel to.

FYI

See the appendix on page 144 for a directory of major North American indie craft shows.

APPLICATION PROCESS

Most of the big craft shows are juried, which means the organizers decide who makes the cut based on an application. The competition is stiff—some shows have acceptance rates rivaling those of Ivy League colleges.

Application

Organizers have a lot of things to consider when choosing who sells at their fair. Is there a good balance of different kinds of crafts? (Jewelry is notoriously over-represented in most application pools, for example.) Is a crafter doing something really unique? Some shows set aside a certain number of tables for newbies each year. Others really love focusing on local talent, like Chicago's DIY Trunk Show, run by the Chicago Craft Mafia. Poise.cc's Cinnamon Cooper, one of the judges, says they don't accept anyone farther than five hours away from Chicago, and about 80 percent of their sellers are in Chicago or its suburbs. "Part of it's logistical," she says. With Chicago's wonderful winter weather, "people coming in from Ohio and Kentucky have had problems and bailed out of the one-day show." Cooper says they also try to keep about 10 to 15 percent of their tables open for newbies, because she and partner Amy Carlton were very green when they started the show.

If you're new to the craft show scene, consider sharing a table with a friend. It can boost your chances of getting in because it's less of a risk for organizers to have two new crafters share a table than to give an entire space to someone who's never sold at a show before. Plus, it boosts the overall diversity of the show. Remember how I said there's always an overflow of jewelry peddlers? If you sell Shrinky-Dink earrings and your friend sells wallets woven from grocery bags, go in on an application together!

Liz Rosino, who started Craftin' Outlaws in Columbus, Ohio, has developed a precise process for selecting crafters. "After the deadline, all the complete applications are sorted into categories, such as jewelry, handbags and paper goods," she says. "It's really important to me to have a large variety of types of items—there are only so many booths for jewelry or bags. Those are probably the most popular categories, so they're the hardest to get a spot in. We even divide it down to people who make beaded jewelry, silver jewelry and so on, to make sure we have no duplicates."

Cooper says she looks for people using unique materials with a special focus on sustainability—economic as well as ecological. "We give extra points to recycled or fair trade items, and look for people who are being paid fair wages," she says.

If you really want to get into a show, the most important thing is to follow application instructions to a T, be on time and use photos that really do justice to your work. (See the tips on taking awesome photos on page 60.)

Rejection

Got turned down by your dream show? Don't get discouraged. Some big shows get up to four times the number of applications they can accept. That means the judging committee has to reject some damn good crafters. Kristen Rask, who runs the sweet store Schmancy in Seattle and works with the Urban Craft Uprising show there, has one common explanation for rejections: "People don't follow directions!" she says. "If you have 500 applicants or more, organizers get nitpicky."

So if the show organizers ask for attached photos, don't send a link. If you have to pay the table fee when you apply, don't let yourself forget! (Table fees are generally returned to non-accepted crafters after the decisions have been made public. Whether there's a nonrefundable fee varies from show to show.)

If you do get the dreaded "thanks but no thanks" e-mail, be gracious. Rask has received some awkward post-rejection messages. "Sometimes people send e-mails saying, 'I'm really disappointed. This is the second year I've been rejected.' I feel bad, but that's no way to make me want to take you as a vendor!"

GETTING PREPPED

Getting that first congratulatory e-mail from the craft show organizer is an exhilarating feeling. And now the real work starts!

Travel arrangements

Aside from tons of your crafts, a table display and other odds and ends, you also have to figure out your travel and lodging arrangements if it's not a local show. (See the craft show profitability worksheet on the next page to help you figure out what you can afford.) Often the organizers will send info on affordable lodging—some even try to match up crafters with local hosts or hotel roommates. It's a good idea to reach out to your Facebook friends to see if any wayward relatives or college buddies live in the area you're visiting. Check the list of crafters selling at the show to see if any live near you, and send them a friendly e-mail to see if they're interested in carpooling. If you've got to go it alone, check sites like Priceline (www.priceline.com) and Kayak (www.kayak.com) for airfare and hotel deals.

Jenny Harada on ...
Bringing Baby

Jenny Harada's kooky stuffed animals (and her babies) have made appearances at craft shows all across the country.

"Bring lots of snacks and toys and activities and a helper. Actually, I would recommend leaving them home if you can! In a way, it's fun to have them there, but it can also be stressful and distracting. If they are old enough to help out, it might be a different story, but I haven't reached that stage yet."

Craft Show Profitability

Is the craft show worth it? If you're looking to make big bucks and that's it, skip the show. If not, use the worksheet below to estimate how profitable a craft show will be for you. It will also help you track your real profits after attending a show.

EXPENSES

Application fee: _____

Table fee: _____

Vendor's license (if applicable): _____

Travel (gas, airfare, parking): _____

Lodging: _____

Food: _____

Other: _____

Total Expenses: _____

Total expenses (B): _____

Total (anticipated) sales (A): _____

NET PROFIT (A–B): _____

Planning for the show

The show organizers will send you some basic information, such as when you should arrive on the day of the show to set up, anything special you need to bring (such as a tent if you'll be outside), and whether you need a local vendor's permit at the show. (But don't assume that if they don't say anything you're in the clear on sales tax. Check the state's department of taxation or revenue for all the rules.) Organizers are generally amazing, multitasking angels, but don't expect them to be able to hold your hand the entire time. Scour the show's Web site and devour all the vendor information you can find. You'll find that most FAQs are answered before you even ask.

If you plan to accept credit cards at the show, make sure there's Wi-Fi access for your laptop. Also, not all shows have electrical outlets for every booth. If you need juice, tell the organizers when you apply, or ask about it when table assignments are made.

If you're bringing a friend along, enlist them well ahead of time and make sure they've got all the info and know whether to request days off work. Having some extra hands is often really helpful, but make sure you compensate them for their time, whether it's in grub, hugs or real cash.

If your crafts are one of a kind, be sure to remove the items you take to the show from your online storefront. Etsy has an option to make items inactive. But make sure your store isn't completely empty! Many crafters report a jump in sales after a craft show.

TABLE DISPLAYS

First impressions are everything at a craft show. If your table is cluttered without a visible business name and no prices to be found, it's the aesthetic equivalent of bad BO.

If you've been to indie craft shows (if you haven't, you need to!), you know that the most popular sellers have the most eye-catching, pretty or unusual table displays. It doesn't take big bucks to make a great setup—all you need is a good imagination and a little planning.

Practice your setup on the kitchen table before you unveil it at a show. Ask a friend to give you feedback, and take pictures so you can replicate the layout on the day of the show.

It's key to think vertically. A table with everything laid out flat doesn't catch anyone's eye from across the room. Use shelves, boxes or stands to create height. Some sellers turn down the table and use room dividers or other completely vertical displays for their wares.

Assuming you're working with the common 8-foot folding table, the cornerstone of your display is the table covering. (Nobody wants to see all that scratched up Masonite.) It should match your biz's look. Is your style utilitarian? Try plain kraft paper or corrugated cardboard. Is your style retro and hip? Go with a patterned bedsheet or curtains. Do you want to surprise visitors with something unusual? Get some Astroturf or bubble wrap! (Get more ideas on page 86.)

Go through your closets and kitchen with new eyes. What could you use for a display? Borrow your roommate's coat rack, clean off the dish rack, or use a stack of cool-looking books as props. Anne Holman displays her silver jewelry in white ceramic dishes. She uses a shallow white bowl filled with red lentils (see page 85) to show off her rings and flat sushi trays for her necklaces.

Kati Hanimägi of Oddball Press displays her letterpress cards and prints on top of stacks of prints that weren't up to snuff. "I knew that I wanted something very papery and utilitarian, so rather than use a tablecloth, I thought rolls of kraft paper would be the best neutral surface to make the product pop," she says. "From there, I drew up a simple little design for some wood racks that would hold three different card styles. I handed off the design to my handy husband, who built ten of them out of scrap wood we had piling up in the basement."

Then she just had to figure out how to set up the racks at different levels. "Originally, I covered hardback books with paper and stacked them up to get different heights for the racks to sit on. It looked good, but there was so much paper waste, and it was a lot of work to schlep around boxes of books." Hanimägi realized she could make use of 750 prints that weren't up to snuff. "I had a whole carton of printed chipboard with no use. As Craftin' Outlaws approached, I had the revelation to use the rejected prints as my risers. They're the most expensive risers I could have created, but I think they pull the booth together."

If you're lucky enough to live near an IKEA, spend a day scouring the Swedish superstore for cheap items you could repurpose to fit your needs. Thrift stores are also full of things you can turn into killer table displays. For example, I got some simple wooden CD crates for 50 cents each from Goodwill. I sanded them and coated them with silver spray paint to make them look flashy; they're the perfect size for displaying my hand-printed cards!

One thing to keep in mind as you're devising a table display is the fact that you'll have to be able to set it up, tear it down and transport it. Annie Chau of Imogene originally wanted to grow her own grass to use in her display but ended up going with Astroturf because it was much more practical. "I need to stay super-modular and mobile for craft shows," she says. The linen necklace busts she uses in her display aren't too bulky and make a great impression. Also make sure your display is weatherproof if you're doing a show outdoors. A disintegrated table display is not a good look.

Aline Yamada of yumi yumi shows off her prints in simple wooden boxes from IKEA.

Anne Holman uses a shallow white bowl filled with red lentils to show off her rings.

Creative Table Coverings

Choose one of these materials for an undoubtably awesome base for your table display.

Casual
gingham tablecloth

Quirky
Astroturf

Basic
kraft paper

Earthy
burlap

Boho
ethnic cloth

Trendy
designer fabric

Urban
sheet metal

Green
old newspaper

Chic
pashmina

DAY OF SHOW

Rise and shine! Today's the big day, and as much as it might suck to be hauling your stuff around at 6 a.m., it's best to be on time. After you get set up, you'll have time to relax, grab a bagel and meet your crafty neighbors.

If you're smart (and since you're reading this book, you obviously are), you'll have gotten everything together the night before the show and checked off everything on the list on page 89. I always make a grocery store trip and a bank run the day before a show to get snacks, drinks and change. (Get snacks that are easy to put down when a customer arrives—go for tidy bite-size things like crackers, grapes or granola bars. This is not the time, nor the place for hot wings.) Also do a quick inventory check the night before the show or before the doors open to make a record of how much stuff you brought with you.

You'll have your table setup down to a science by this point, so when you arrive at the show, you'll be able to check in and get started right away. Look for an organizer or volunteer when you arrive to get registered and find your table.

Introduce yourself to your crafty neighbors! I've met a lot of awesome people—and new friends—at indie craft shows. If nothing else, your tablemates will be the folks you turn to when you gotta make a restroom run. Most next-door neighbors are happy to watch your table for a sec if you offer to do the same.

Before you know it, the doors will open and you'll be flooded with curious customers! Don't be freaked about dealing with the

FYI

One of the big upsides of traveling for shows is that you can build up your brand in other cities where people might not know your stuff. So, be sure everyone leaves your table with a sticker or business card with your name and URL on it.

public—people dig that they get to interact with crafters. Say hello to everyone who stops by your table, even if you doubt they'll buy anything. One great way to engage potential buyers is to share something about your technique. For example, when I see someone pick up a blank journal I made, I'll tell them the paper inside is all salvaged vintage stock. The most important thing is to stay friendly, even if your feet are killing you and you've been running all day on just a veggie dog. Standing behind your table makes you much more approachable than if you're sitting slouched with your arms crossed. Resist the temptation to work on your knitting when business is slow. Nothing says "I don't want to be here" more than a crafter paying more attention to her needles than her potential customers.

If you've got to collect sales tax, have a cheat sheet by your cash box for easy calculating. Having a calculator is handy, but why do the same multiplication dozens of times? Make sure everybody who buys from you signs up for your mailing list, which should be prominently displayed on your table on a clipboard with a functioning pen. Encourage everybody—even non-buyers—to take a sticker, business card or other freebie. Know where the nearest ATM is to be able to help cash-strapped shoppers. Some crafters don't take checks, but I generally do and haven't been burned yet. Ask to see the buyer's ID, and ask her to write her phone number on the check just in case. If you accept credit cards, always check the expiration date and for a signature on the back.

If you've got a friend with you to watch the table (or friendly neighbors) take time to walk around the show, meet other crafters and collect business cards. You can get a few new names for your blogroll, trade cross-stitching tips and make some friends while you're at it.

Though you might feel like you're running yourself ragged, take time to enjoy the ambience. Have you ever been surrounded by so many incredible, creative people in your life? This is enough to get me charged up and dancing behind my table even when I'm dog tired. If you're lucky, the show will have a DJ to keep you pumped the whole day.

Day-of-Show Checklist

FOR YOUR BOOTH

- [ ] more crafts than you think you'll need
- [ ] kickass table display
- [ ] sturdy totes, boxes or bags to transport your goods
- [ ] price tags and signs
- [ ] sign or banner with your business name
- [ ] business cards
- [ ] freebies (stickers, pins, flyers)
- [ ] e-mail sign-up list
- [ ] cash box
- [ ] table and chair if you have to supply your own
- [ ] tent if needed
- [ ] mirror if you're selling clothes, accessories or jewelry
- [ ] lighting if needed
- [ ] bags for customers (as simple as recycled grocery bags or as fancy as custom screen-printed paper bags)
- [ ] scissors, tape and pins

- [ ] pens, notebook, paper
- [ ] $50+ in small bills for change
- [ ] calculator
- [ ] your laptop or other credit card processing equipment
- [ ] book of sales receipts

FOR YOU

- [ ] water and other drinks
- [ ] layers of clothing
- [ ] sunscreen if you're outside
- [ ] aspirin, bandages, first-aid supplies and your regular meds
- [ ] snacks
- [ ] charged cell phone
- [ ] comfortable shoes
- [ ] wipes and/or anti-bacterial gel
- [ ] map and parking information

Caitlin Phillips on ...
Sealing the Deal

Caitlin Phillips is the mastermind behind Rebound Designs, a purveyor of book purses. She sells her wares at craft shows around the country as well as at Washington, D.C.'s weekly Eastern Market, so she knows sales.

"When you're trying to make a sale, you want to avoid the word 'no.' When you greet people, never ask 'Can I help you with anything?' or 'Is there anything I can help you with?' Instead say, 'If you have any questions, let me know.' You want to ask your potential customers open-ended questions.

"When someone says, 'Oh, your stuff is so pretty!' it's really tempting to say, 'Thank you.' But 'thank you' actually signals the end of the transaction. You don't want to say this until they're handing you money. Instead say, 'I'm so glad you like it!' Show them why that item is special, how you made it or how to use it.

"You should practice your answers to any objections your customers might have. The right response to 'it's not in my size' is always 'I can make it in your size!' If someone says, 'That's too expensive,' try to figure out if they mean it's too expensive for them, or if they think it's not worth the money. If it's the former, suggest an item in a lower price range. If it's the latter, explain your process and how your goods are worth the money.

"When you're about to close the sale, stay friendly and upbeat. Try, 'Did you want to go ahead and get that?' or 'Did you want to do cash or charge?' And when you seal the deal, make sure to say thanks!"

THE POSTMORTEM

And that's a wrap! You've made it through the show, hopefully with a lot of sales, some new friends and a new appreciation for salespeople.

Watch other crafters to see when they start tearing down their tables—most will begin collecting their things right at closing time. Leaving a craft show early is considered very bad etiquette, especially if you just peace-out without saying anything to the organizer. The organizers will likely close the doors at the exact time the show's slated to end, but there will be a few last-minute shoppers making the rounds.

I find it really helpful to take inventory of my stock after the show to see what sold best and figure out if I broke even. Keeping track helps me be better prepared for my next show, and I can craft to meet demand. For example, I know my notebooks in the $8 to $15 range always sell out, so I try to beef up my stock of those. Make some general notes about your experience, too: Were the crowds good? Were the organizers organized? Would you want to do the show again?

Once you've sold at a few different shows, you might re-evaluate your pricing strategy, too. Miss Chief Productions' Jessica Manack, one of the organizers of Pittsburgh's Handmade Arcade, heard mixed reviews from some vendors at one show. "A few people from bigger cities said they weren't selling a lot of stuff. That's likely because they were charging New York prices, like $36 for a baby T-shirt," she says. "We wondered if we should let people know that Pittsburgh prices aren't that high."

Be sure to thank the organizers and let them know how your day went. If that means pointing out some shortcomings, do it diplomatically. Being courteous goes a long way, says Kristen Rask. "One woman was really rude at the end of the show, so we reconsidered when she applied the next year," Rask says. "It's not like you have to kiss everyone's ass, but if you're gracious, you'll be remembered."

DIY CRAFT SHOWS

No show? If you live hundreds of miles from the nearest indie craft show or simply see room for a new kind of scene, start your own! It can't be done fast, but it can be done with a little money and a lot of elbow grease.

"We didn't realize how much work it'd be when we first started, and we didn't know how big it would be," Cinnamon Cooper says about the DIY Trunk Show. She and partner Amy Carlton thought they'd just find a room somewhere in Chicago and have a small show. Then they found the cavernous Pulaski Park Auditorium and fell in love with it. "I said, 'Oh my god, we have to have the show here.' We measured out how many people would fill it—32 people. 'Can we find 32 crafters? I don't know, let's try!'" By putting up messages on crafty community Web sites they had the show's roster full within a month. "It was just complete luck," she says.

Faythe Levine's first show as a seller was Renegade Chicago. "It was an important turning point for me. I loved the energy, loved the interaction and sense of community," she says. After the show, she came home to Milwaukee and wanted to create something like Renegade in her hometown. At the time, she was posting daily on the Switchboards, Get Crafty and Craftster, and word of mouth helped get Art vs. Craft going. "The biggest challenge was working with a space and the logistics of traffic flow and how many people you can fit," Levine says. "It's taken me almost five years to find a space that works and the number of vendors that's good. We had a couple disaster spatial issues, with someone being put in a weird spot or misjudging the space."

> **IT WAS AN IMPORTANT TURNING POINT FOR ME. I LOVED THE ENERGY, LOVED THE INTERACTION AND SENSE OF COMMUNITY.**
>
> —FAYTHE LEVINE

Levine focuses all her advertising efforts locally. "We do local radio spots and print ads with local weeklies. I plaster all the hot spots where the audience is going to be with hand-screened posters and postcards," she says. The Little Friends of Printmaking—a sweet Milwaukee-based design studio—has created the promo materials for the last few years. She's also traded with a natural food store—swapping ad space in the Art vs. Craft flier for window graphics. "It's my demographic, so it's like having a billboard up in a grocery store," she says. "I try to think of places where the people who'd go to my show go. Can that business benefit from my show? How can we all help each other? It's not just about promoting Art vs. Craft but about the longevity of local business in Milwaukee."

Cinnamon Cooper on ...
Sponsorship

"I think it's a really fine line between DIY and selling out. When you look for sponsors, there are businesses just trying to capitalize on the movement that's already been created, trying to tie their brand with your vision. But on the other hand, there are businesses like O'Reilly Media, a publisher that's sustainable and starting to be profitable. It's up to each crafter or organizer to figure out how their brand identity and personal beliefs and business correspond with the business they're teaming up with. I have no problem with going to CRAFT and trading a blog post for putting out fliers and cards. I know they're going after the same market I am in the same way I am, trying to spread knowledge and not just latch onto the image I've created."

Across the country in Seattle, the organizers of Urban Craft Uprising gave attendees a survey to see what potential customers wanted in terms of wares and prices. Kristen Rask, the marketing director for the show, uses a blog and newsletters to keep in touch with fans and vendors throughout the year. "The awesome thing about having big shows is that there are a lot of vendors to talk about it," she says. "Word of mouth helps get some big names!" Urban Craft Uprising has craft book author signings during the show, which allows for cross-promotion with local bookstores.

Organize your show in 13 steps

1. Find a venue. What can you afford? How many crafters will the space fit? Will anyone give you a deal? (Ask at coffee shops, bars, parks, churches, art galleries, fairgrounds, community centers, etc.) Is there adequate parking? Is there a lot of room for foot traffic?

2. Pick a name. Don't pick one that's already taken and don't play off an established show's name, like "Crafty NoCal Bastards" or "Renegade Craft Show 2: Electric Boogaloo."

3. Organize the business side. Set up a checking account for just the show, and check to see if you need any city permits or insurance. Figure out your costs (space rental, table rental, permits) and determine how much you need to charge per table. Keep in mind that the most common table size is 8' (2m) long and the usual tent space is 10' × 10' (3m × 3m).

4. Determine a date. Saturdays or Sundays are usually ideal. If you're planning to have your show outdoors, setting your date between May and September is best. Holiday shows garner a lot of traffic, so consider an indoor date in November or December.

5. Create an Internet presence. Something as simple as having a blog devoted to the show will give you some credibility and help people who google for your show.

6. Enlist crafters. Post information about your show in the related forums in craft community Web sites and alert your local Craft Mafia. You could invite crafters, do a juried show or just accept everyone until you're full.

7. Find sponsors. Make the show a community affair. Find sponsors to help defray the financial burden, and sell ads in your program. Create a few levels of sponsorship (for example, $20 for a small ad in the program or $200 for a banner on-site) to give potential backers options. Look locally, but also approach businesses that serve the craft community.

8. Find helpers. Enlist a friend to be the DJ for the day—it helps keep energy up! If you get volunteers for the day of the show, they can help you organize the crafters, give them breaks, answer questions from visitors and manage traffic.

9. Send all the details to your crafters. Let them know when to arrive, where to park, where there's food available, lodging suggestions and directions, for example.

10. Advertise and promote the show. E-mail local newspapers, Web sites, TV and radio stations and magazines. Send personal invites to movers and shakers in the craft world. If you can afford it, buy an ad in your local alternative weekly, or try bartering—offer ad space in your show program in exchange for ad space in their paper. Same goes for a local printer! Make signage and banners for the venue, so passersby are drawn into the show.

11. Create a program. This can be a simple photocopied flier or a saddle-stitched multipage deal. It should include a directory of crafters with a map, information about you and the show, and ads from any sponsors you have.

12. Get set up. If possible, arrange the tables and chairs the night before the show. On the day of, arrive before the crafters to make sure everything's in line for a great day.

13. Open the doors! It's going to be hella busy, but it'll be so worth it. Check in with the crafters periodically, and enjoy your position as a crafty ambassador. Congratulations, you're now a pillar of the craft community!

Chapter 5
Get Noticed

You're flipping through the latest issue of *Venus Zine*, and the fantastic crafts you see inspire a little jealousy. How did those people get in the magazine? How much would it cost to buy an ad? How come nobody knows how awesome your crafts are yet? You can start the coolest craft biz in the world, but no one will ever know about it unless you start tooting your own horn.

You won't need to hire a public relations rep to get the word out, at least not off the bat. There's plenty you can do on your own and on the cheap to promote your business. All you need is an Internet connection and a little moxie. We're gonna show you how to get noticed, get customers coming back and get good press. Go get 'em!

BE YOUR OWN PR PERSON

"Self-promotion has been the most difficult thing for me. I'm a very shy person, and painfully so when it comes to talking about my own work," jewelry maker Samantha Lopez says. "Perhaps the most valuable lesson I've learned is to have the ability to see what I do as not only my passion but also my job. Detaching myself from it in a way has made everything much easier to handle."

The first step to becoming your own PR person is to develop your elevator pitch. How would you describe your business, in just a few seconds, to someone you've never met? For example, when people ask me what I'm writing my book about, I tell them, "It's a how-to business book for part-time indie crafters." It might need some explaining, sure, to someone unfamiliar with the scene, but if a pitch spurs questions, that's great—you've got them hooked.

Online tactics

Start a blog, if you don't already have one. It's a great (and free) way to show your work and create relationships with your customers. It's a good way to build a following, especially if you post freebies like tutorials or desktop wallpaper and pretty photos of what you're working on.

"I don't do much promotion other than blogging," says Jesse Breytenbach, a printmaker in South Africa. "I spend a lot of time reading other blogs and commenting on them. Not that I do it as promotion—I do it because it's great to be part of the community. Whenever a new person comments on my blog, I have a look at theirs and often add it to my links. I love that I've made blog friends this way—they've bought from me, and I've bought from them, too." She's also been contacted by people in publishing in South Africa who see items on her blog that they include in their magazines.

If you're going to do the blog thing, keep in mind these essetials:

- Post at least once a week—but several times a week is even better.
- Let readers get to know you.
- But don't get too personal.
- Use lots of pictures!
- Don't use the blog solely for self-promotion.
- Always spell-check.

Blog Platforms

These are the most popular and user-friendly blogging tools:

Blogger (www.blogger.com): Easy to use; free but with limited customization; up to 300 MB of storage.

LiveJournal (www.livejournal.com): More like a personal journal; free basic account; $19.95/year paid account includes 2 GB of storage.

MovableType (www.movabletype.com): More of a content management system; can be used to build Web sites as well as blogs; basic account is free.

Typepad (www.typepad.com): Lots of options for blog experts; basic account is $4.95/month and includes 100 MB of storage.

Wordpress (www.wordpress.com): Very customizable; free account includes 3 GB of storage; premium account offers more options.

Taryn Hipp uses blogs as well as social networking sites to promote MyMy.us. Set up a Twitter account for your biz (or just incorporate a little self-promotion into your personal feed). You can also create a Facebook page for your brand and invite your customers to join. Reward your followers with special coupon codes and early-bird opportunities.

Hipp does say that although she uses blogs and social networking sites as well as magazine advertising to promote her business, the real results come from something much more simple. "The number one thing is just doing what you do well. It's amazing what a happy customer will do for you," she says. "Being a nice person and loving what you do is reflected in your business. You can spend thousands of dollars on print ads and promotions and postcards, but if you're not sending out orders on time, it won't matter."

Other PR opportunities

An awesome way to get noticed is to contribute to the Sampler (www.homeofthesampler.com), a monthly mailer started by the indubitable Marie Kare and now run by Etsy. Craft admirers subscribe to the Sampler to get a priority mail box full of awesome stuff each month. Indie businesses send in samples of their products and promotional materials in exchange for one of that month's Samplers, promotion on the Web site and exposure to media types. You can contribute as few as 25 pieces or hundreds if you have 'em! The more samples you send in, the better deals you get for promotion.

You obviously don't want to send in 25 items that you usually sell for $50 apiece, but you could contribute, say, 48 $5 items and two big-ticket items for the luck of the draw. Be sure to package your items nicely and include your contact info somewhere. Lots of media folks use the Sampler to stay abreast of craft trends, so put your most crafty foot forward!

Then there are the PR opportunities that seem fantastic, but really aren't, like getting offers to participate in celebrity gift bags. Considering that it can cost hundreds—often thousands—of dollars to get your stuff into a gift tent and total exposure isn't guaranteed, it's probably not a worthwhile investment.

DIRECT MAIL

Direct e-mail is perhaps the best and easiest way to drum up sales. Collect the e-mail addresses of anyone who buys stuff from you and have a sign-up area on your Web site and a sheet at craft shows.

Make it clear that you won't sell their addresses or use them for anything other than periodic messages from you. If someone asks to be removed from your list, do it promptly and without argument. Using an e-marketing service (see below) will give recipients easy subscription options. A really low-tech way to do a mailing list is to simply create a list of contacts within your e-mail account and BCC everybody when you send out a message.

Send out a message every month or so to remind people that you're still around. Let readers know what you've been up to, what new projects you've been working on, the newest items in your shop and where you'll be selling this season. Make it personal—don't just blatantly market to them.

Jessica Manack, who uses NotifyList for periodic Miss Chief Productions mailings, says there is a limit to a customer's attention. "A girl I know sent out her mailing list twice a week. It was so annoying," she says. "When we send one out, at least one previous customer will come back and buy something. I think four to six mailings a year is optimal."

E-mail Newsletter Services

Emma: www.myemma.com
Starting at $30/month, plus $99 setup fee

NotifyList: www.notifylist.com
Free

Constant Contact: www.constantcontact.com
Starting at $15/month

GETTING PRESS

The most important thing is to target media outlets whose customer base overlaps your own. Just as *Feminist Photocopied Quarterly* probably isn't interested in bedazzled "Born to Shop" onesies, *Super Glossy Magazine* doesn't give a lot of space to hemp tampon ornaments.

After you've identified a blog or magazine you think would be a good fit, figure out who to send your press release or samples to. With big magazines, addressing parcels to the editor-in-chief usually lands them in the hands of the editorial assistants. With some googling, you can usually figure out which of the mid-level editors is in charge of the products department, and directing your submission to them will yield the best results. Many magazines also list their product submission guidelines on their Web sites. Some prefer mailed submissions only; others only consider e-mailed pitches. Jenny Hart of Sublime Stitching recommends sending samples over hackneyed press releases. If you do send a sample, don't expect to see it again. Magazine staffs have much better things to do than return all the unsolicited materials they receive.

Blogs' turnaround times for product features are understandably shorter than magazines'. You might be OK sending a Valentine's Day press release to a blog the week before, but *Super Glossy Magazine*'s February issue went to press months ago. As a rule of thumb, pitch time-sensitive products to magazines six months in advance. That way you'll stand a chance of hitting the editor's desk just as she's starting to brainstorm ideas for that issue. Also, consider pitching to regional magazines and newspapers that might be interested in what a local crafter is doing. They may not be as fancy, but you stand a much better chance at getting coverage.

Consider including a press section on your Web site where you can park press releases and high-res, print-quality photos ready for downloading. It'll make life easier for everyone.

Grace Bonney on ...
Press Releases

Grace Bonney knows good craft when she sees it. Her blog, Design*Sponge (www.designspongeonline.com) features dozens of innovative designs every day that she finds by scouring the Internet constantly and reading more press releases than anybody in her right mind should. She shares some of her preferences and advice for up-and-coming crafters.

What do you look for in a press release?
"Two words: short and direct. I read close to a thousand press releases a week. For me, a good press release is a simple, digital document that gets right to the point. Write a short intro that tells me who you are, then get straight to the good stuff: what you're making or selling, how much it costs, and why it's special. Attach a few good photos, and that's it. A great press release should rely on the strength of the product, not the personal life of the designer behind it."

What turns you off?
"Sob stories. People tell me about parents or pets that have died and that 'writing about my product would really make my day and I really need this right now.' How am I supposed to say no to that? And if I do, I feel like a real jerk. I know life and work are intertwined, but it's really best to leave personal stories out until you've established some sort of personal relationship. Press should happen because of a great product, not a guilt trip."

What do you wish more crafters knew about publicity?
"Photography is about 80 percent of the battle. Great photos say way more than a press release ever could. When I get a submission, the first thing I do is scroll down to look at pictures. If those grab me, I hardly need to read anything else. Other than that, it's good to know that short and sweet is always best. You can elaborate in the follow-up."

Do and don'ts of dealing with magazines

Speaking from my own experience as a magazine editor, here are some guidelines to follow when contacting and working with magazines.

DO read a copy or two of the magazine before submitting stuff to customize the pitch.

DON'T call. Most editors prefer e-mail or snail mail.

DO send samples to as many magazines as are applicable.

DON'T CC every contact you have on a generic e-mail. It's a surefire way to get deleted.

DO take time to formulate a thoughtful response to an editor's e-mail. Sending something right away and then retracting it in a follow-up is confusing.

DON'T take three weeks to respond to an editor's request. You might miss the boat entirely!

DO send requested materials on time and in the format your contact requested.

DON'T be late. If you can't avoid it, apologize in a professional manner—that means no gruesome details or excuses.

DO condense any questions into one e-mail.

DON'T send six e-mails over the course of the night as you think of more things you want to ask.

DO ask for a contributor's copy of the issue you appear in.

DON'T call every week asking if your piece has run yet.

DO scan your clips and post them on your Web site

FYI

Need to find *Super Glossy Magazine*'s market editor's e-mail address? Go to Mastheads.org, a site with contact information for practically every magazine out there. Access starts at $4 a week.

Press Release Template

Contact person (that's you)
Title, company
Phone number
E-mail address

FOR IMMEDIATE RELEASE

Eye-catching, descriptive summary/headline

City, State (Date)—First paragraph states the main news.

Second paragraph gives more details.

Third paragraph includes a quote from a person involved with the project.

Fourth paragraph gives any additional details and information.

###

ABOUT: Describe the history of your company, your reach and what you do.

Attach two or three awesome Web-quality photos and indicate that print-quality images are available.

ADVERTISING

Buying ads in magazines can be expensive, with no guarantee of return. But at the same time, if you advertise in the right venue, such as a magazine that supports indie crafters, it can get your Web site a lot of hits.

Before you think about slapping down the big bucks for a piece of real estate in *Super Glossy Magazine*, make sure your target audience is the magazine's target audience, too. For example, I often visit dozens of the Web sites advertised in magazines such as *BUST, Venus Zine* and *ReadyMade* because I know they're likely to be women-operated, indie and awesome.

You can find rates for ads on a publication's Web site; look for keywords such as *advertising* or *media kit* to take you to the right spot. You might have to e-mail an ad rep to get the exact prices and deadlines. Some magazines offer discounted rates for indie businesses—it never hurts to ask!

If you do buy ad space, you'll have to supply the ad's image to the magazine. You'll get exact specs when you contact a rep. This is the time to ask a graphic designer friend to help you out if you're not an Adobe Illustrator genius. Browse through the magazine's ads and see what other people are doing, what you like or dislike and what grabs your attention.

Because advertising space isn't so cheap, a good tactic is to share the ad with some crafty friends or people from your local Craft Mafia. Sometimes you can find people on crafty message boards seeking partners to buy ad space together.

Another cheaper option is to advertise on magazines' Web sites. The rates are generally lower than they are for print ads. Craft-focused Web sites and blogs also offer ad space for indie businesses. Which of the sites you visit on a daily basis are ad-supported? Do a little digging to find their rates or at least their ad coordinator.

The real grassroots route is to trade links with other crafters. Most crafters' Web sites have a page for links to other like-minded shops. (If you don't have one, you should make one!) Usually, if you e-mail crafters you admire and ask to trade links, they'll be happy to oblige! Some crafters even use banner or button ads for trading. Ask your designer buddy to whip something up for you in Illustrator.

10 Ways to Kick-Start Your Sales

1. Give an item to a popular craft blog or Web site for a giveaway.

2. Put your store URL in your e-mail signature.

3. Offer coupons to repeat customers. Keep 'em coming back for more!

4. Give a gift certificate to the fan who creates the best YouTube video about your products.

5. Create a tag or a pool on Flickr for customers to use to post pictures of themselves with your goods.

6. Put links to your store in all your social networking profiles.

7. Offer free shipping for a limited time with a minimum purchase.

8. Include cool swag with every shipment (buttons, stickers, stuff like that).

9. Create a coupon code exclusively for your friends on MySpace, Facebook, Twitter or Flickr.

10. Post about new items in your blog once a week. (If it's regular, people will come to anticipate your latest offerings!)

Chapter 6
Finding Balance

Once you become a pillar of indie industry, you've gotta deal with a lot of stuff—balancing your real job and crafty job, maintaining a personal life, and dealing with unexpected changes. What if you need to take a break from your biz? What if you want to go full time and become an even bigger crafty superstar? What if you just don't know how to deal with this adorably gory crochet monster you created?

You're not alone. Whatever your deal, I guarantee another crafter has gone through the same thing. That's why having a creative support group is so important: surrounding yourself with people who can offer advice (or at least a shoulder to cry on) is vital to your crafty survival. Whether you're trying to transition to full-time crafting, considering closing up shop or just trying to stay afloat, we'll get you through it!

WORKING FOR A LIVING

Living a crafty double life can be hella tough. It seems like a good deal—you slave away from 9 to 5 (or 4 to midnight) in exchange for a steady paycheck and health insurance, and the rest of the day is yours for the crafting! But what it really comes down to is you working 24-7. How do those crafty superstars handle it?

Jessica Manack balances a very full-time job with running the Miss Chief shop and working on Pittsburgh's Handmade Arcade, which is a job unto itself. "Some Handmade Arcade staffers have jobs where they can send e-mails or work on Etsy during the day, but I can't. So I have to work on things when I get home," she says. She uses Ta-da List (www.tadalist.com) to keep track of things she thinks of during the day. "I love making lists, and I was doing that on sheets of paper, making huge lists that I'd then forget at work."

Although she stays organized, Manack feels like she could do more. "I notice people with spring lines and making a big deal about launching new products. When you're doing it part-time, it's hard to think strategically about your brand," she says. "I feel like I do a lot of just getting by. When I get home, I fill my orders and keep it going, but I just don't have the time or resources to think about expanding because my time's kind of maxed out. I get e-mails from all kinds of stores and galleries who want to carry my stuff, but I just can't do it."

Holly Klump previously worked 20 hours a week so she could do more with misshawklet, but she just bought a house and now she's back to full-time work. "Before, I could do the poor artist thing, but now with the house I need to work full time. It's hard to come home and find some kind of creative energy," she says. "My job isn't the most creative in the world. I'm still trying to find a balance, even though I've been doing it for a while."

Kristen Rask juggles running her store, Schmancy, and working on Urban Craft Uprising and Plush You, plus other projects. "With the economy, I'm like, 'Maybe I should get a job…' But when would that happen? I feel like if I had a job, I would get bitter and mad." One thing that helps Rask stay organized is setting production goals. "When I'm getting ready for a show, I decide what I want to make and how many of each. Then I plot it out with a calendar to see how many things I have to make per week until the show happens. It really helps!"

During slow times, she stockpiles things so she never gets too stressed out. "I'm at the store five days a week at least, and I try to do all the computer stuff at work," Rask says. "I have a no-computer rule at home. That really helps, because when I'm finally at home, I can just craft, be leisurely and try to make new things and not think that I have to make something for money. That helps create new ideas."

In Cleveland, Kati Hanimägi has a more flexible schedule. "I work at my job-job three afternoons a week. Those mornings are spent taking care of e-mail, paying bills, sending invoices and ordering supplies for Oddball Press," she says. "When I have time off, I devote full workdays to my crafty life. I start my crafty day at 9 a.m., break for lunch and walk the dog, and work until 5:30 or 6 p.m." Working out of her home helps her get down to business without ever getting stuck in rush-hour traffic. "I stick to a schedule, although I do have times when I need to work late to meet a deadline or if I'm on a creative roll," she says. "My job-job is a good balance for me because it requires my time and attention while there. I don't need to take it home. But I carry my Oddball life with me all the time, worrying about this or that, thinking of text for a new card, wondering about my next marketing move."

FYI

Making lists can help you stay motivated and organized when you're feeling overwhelmed. I break down the most daunting tasks into easy, bite-size chunks. For example, "make 50 notebooks" is daunting, and I'm likely to procrastinate. But "buy more chiyogami paper," "cut out covers from bookbinder's board" and "collect paper for notebook signatures" are very doable.

MAINTAINING A PERSONAL LIFE

So you've figured out how to balance your day job and your crafty job. But what about your friends and your family—you know, those people you share a bathroom with. If you don't take time to chillax with the people you love, your crafty business will just get you down.

Conflicts and priorities

Jessica Manack feels lucky to live with a kindred spirit. "I think it helps to have a partner who's understanding. I live with someone who's crazy in the same way I am," she says. "He understands the benefit of my spending time on crafting."

Handmade Nation's Faythe Levine sometimes can't tell her personal life and her crafty life apart. "I work all the time," she says. "Learning how to say no to people when I don't have time for something has been a really big lesson for me. And I'm still trying to grasp it." She also tries to be conscious of the people around her. "Like noticing that craft supplies are taking over the house, or every weekend of the summer's been spent at a craft show." This way you can mediate any conflicts before they happen.

And remember to make time for your non-crafty passions. I try to get to my local yoga studio once a week (though I'm currently in a very dry spell). And know when to throw in the towel. The big craft show is the same weekend as a friend's wedding and your dad's birthday? You could make it, if you drive up to see Dad for an hour, immediately go to the show and then sneak out for the nuptials ... Don't do it!

Crafty support groups

If you reach out to other crafters, you'll likely find folks that are happy to give support and advice and help out a fellow maker. Crafters are unique in that, although we're running small businesses in a small market, we don't see each other as competition. Part of this is because of the handmade aspect—none of us are making the exact same things.

Joining local groups, such as a Craft Mafia, is a great way to keep abreast of trends and happenings. Plus, you'll have somebody to talk to when your non-crafty friends get tired of hearing you drone on about your beeswax.

Annie Chau is part of Baltimore's Charm City Craft Mafia. "Everyone who's a part of the Mafia runs a craft business. We share all kinds of information with each other—what shows are coming up, press opportunities, suppliers, business advice, anything you can think of," she says. "The Mafia puts on two craft shows a year and organizes an array of crafty events. I took a sabbatical from the Mafia this year because I simply couldn't balance all of the responsibilities of being a Mafia member with my work."

In South Africa, Jesse Breytenbach meets up with other Cape Town Etsy sellers and collaborates on projects with them. "I also co-run a craft group that meets once a month at a local bookstore," she says. "While I don't actively promote my items there, we all talk about what we do, and I've made some good contacts there—people who work for magazines as stylists, photographers, journalists. And I've met some of my blog buddies there in person, which strengthens the sense of community."

Poise.cc's Cinnamon Cooper along with Amy Carlton created Chicago's DIY Trunk Show; then the Chicago Craft Mafia took over planning the show. "Almost everybody in the Mafia was a vendor at the first show. I had heard about the Austin Craft Mafia online, and I'd felt isolated when I wasn't doing craft shows. I contacted some other people who were really into it," she says. "They thought the Austin Craft Mafia was doing exactly what they wanted to do. I was really grateful for Austin's support."

In 2008, Cooper attended Craft Con in San Francisco, thinking that she was going to stop working on the DIY Trunk Show. But, "I left that weekend thinking, 'Of course I'm going to do this again!' I still think about the conversations I had with people," she says. "People came up to me who I had inspired—it must be how Jenny Hart feels, having inspired people by sharing information. I've gotten so much great information from people I've never met, I feel kind of obligated to keep paying the knowledge forward to as many people as I can."

Many crafters have long-standing friendships and still have never met. Cooper and Megan Reardon of crafty blog Not Martha have never met in person but regularly give each other pep talks. "I was trying to find a certain kind of interfacing a while back, and she was looking for something similar, and we sent each other examples," she says. "Someday we'll meet up."

If you're not in a major metro area, you can find support in online forums such as the Switchboards and Craftster (and I bet you're already lurking on at least one of them). See the appendix on page 132 for a full list of online craft communities.

Holly Klump landed on the Get Crafty forum via Not Martha in 2003. "If I hadn't found that site, I don't think I would have pursued building my own Web site," she says. "I was into bookmaking then, but it never occurred to me that I could do it on my own until I found other people who had similar things going on online." She started consigning with online shops that were recommended to her by another forum member. "Those boards were my first client base. Most of us are connected online and many crafters have personal blogs, so you feel like you know them. I think that's why it [indie craft] is more intimate than regular business. It's more about a community."

Susie Ghahremani of boygirlparty was on Craftster and Get Crafty in the early days of the online DIY scene. "Jenny Kwok from Cut + Paste [www.cutxpaste.com] was one of my first retailers—and continues to be one of my beloved retailers to this day—which was hugely encouraging and helpful as a beginning crafter with no exposure," she says. "All my fellow crafters were pretty much amazing. While many have moved on or changed paths, those crafters will always hold a very special place in my heart!"

TAKING STOCK

Your business is constantly growing and evolving. Even if you're not planning to expand, it's a good policy to re-evaluate your business on a regular basis. Nothing ever stays the same!

Part of the challenge is learning to accept constructive criticism. The business is your baby, but mother doesn't necessarily always know best. "If you care about your business and improving it, you have to keep your ears open to what your customers are saying. After all, if they're taking the time to give you feedback about their experience, it means they care about you improving and making changes and that they're invested enough in remaining a client to see if you can change the experience they had," Sublime Stitching's Jenny Hart says. "It can be tough if that criticism is coming from an unhappy customer. Nobody really likes to hear criticism, but you'll do yourself a huge favor by setting aside your pride and listening. Then it gets easier to take, and it also gets easier to discern the constructive criticism from the unconstructive. What concerns me the most is a customer who has a disappointing experience and doesn't share it with us. Then we don't have the opportunity to address the problem and make it right."

When taking advice from advisers or experts, it can be tougher to determine whether the information is good. "If you're starting out, you can easily be confronted by people with more experience in business who don't necessarily understand how their knowledge applies to what you do. In other words, just because someone approaches you as knowing more about business, it doesn't mean they can offer you valuable advice," Hart says. "Some warning signs are that a person immediately dives into telling you what you should be doing before they've spent any serious time evaluating your business or understanding your goals."

Once, a dude started telling Hart what to do with her five-year-old company within the first five minutes of their conversation. "I listened politely and considered his advice, but I recognized it as not applicable to my business model. You should never apply advice that you don't understand or work with an adviser who doesn't speak to you in ways that make perfect sense to you."

That doesn't mean you should discount an adviser who is unfamiliar with the craft scene. "One of my most trusted advisers is someone with years of business experience but no direct relation to the DIY movement, needlework or crafting. He didn't start offering advice before he'd spent several hours listening to me talk about my business model, my customers and my goals," Hart says. "The types of questions he asked about my business were how I knew he 'got it.' He offered advice in our first meeting that I had never before considered, but it made sense to me and I could apply it immediately and see results from it. Those were all indicators that I was dealing with a valuable adviser."

> IF YOU CARE ABOUT YOUR BUSINESS, YOU HAVE TO KEEP YOUR EARS OPEN TO WHAT YOUR CUSTOMERS ARE SAYING. AFTER ALL, IF THEY'RE TAKING THE TIME TO GIVE YOU FEEDBACK IT MEANS THEY CARE ABOUT YOU IMPROVING.
>
> –JENNY HART

CHANGES

Along the path of crafty business, you might take wrong turns. My My's Taryn Hipp totally cops to a scheme that didn't work out. In 2006, she was walking the dogs and saw an empty storefront. Within two weeks, she was signing the lease. "I had no financial backing, no business plan, nothing. There was an empty space and I wanted it," she says. "It was only open for about nine months."

Hipp can think of a couple reasons why the consignment shop wasn't successful. "Mostly it was just the wrong place at the wrong time, and I rushed into it," she says. "But I don't regret it at all. I don't think I've ever been happier. Every morning I'd

Taking It Down a Notch

Has your part-time crafting become so big-time that you never see your friends? Or maybe it's not so much successful as it is stressful. When crafting takes over your life, it's time for some more of that self-reflection stuff: Are you happy doing what you're doing? Are you having fun with it? And, the big one: Do you want to keep doing it?

It's hard to see something come to an end, but it's true that nothing ever stays the same. Maybe you're moving to a new city, having a baby or going back to school. Or maybe you got carpal tunnel from crocheting so many amigurumi. Or maybe you decided that you just don't want to craft for profit anymore.

So stop. (After you've resolved all your outstanding orders and debts, of course.) If you're left with a massive amount of stuff, unload your leftover stock in a blowout sale. You can give your materials to other crafters in trades, or sell them on Etsy—they have a category especially for materials.

walk up to my store and unlock the door and turn the lights on. It was really the best day, every day."

"I kind of always knew it was a losing battle. But at the same time, I believed in it so much, and in my consigners and the community, that even though it was financially draining, I still wanted to keep it up," Hipp says. "We were holding classes, and we had a zine library. We had parties and sidewalk sales." Local artists would walk in off the street, looking to sell their work. "I was having such a good time, but I kept ignoring the fact that it was impossible to continue," she says. "But to the day I closed, I still believed it could work."

Hipp tried to keep the Web site running for a while after the store closed but fell behind with it and realized she had to regroup. "It was a really humbling feeling. I didn't want people to see me failing. And I didn't want to let down my consigners," she says. "But I would never tell someone not to open a store." Hipp also advises, "It's important to remember the joy you get from crafting."

Hipp relaunched MyMy.us in December 2008. "I'm back in it 24-7. If I'm not at work or sleeping, I'm consumed by it. It makes me happy," she says. "But I also know I need to have that happy medium of having a social life and not being completely engrossed in this thing." She works the morning shift, so she can devote the rest of her day to things that keep her balanced. But it helps that everyone in her life is creative. "Even if I'm not making something, I'm at a friend's house doing something or I'm at a show. I'm taking part in some kind of creative endeavor, which makes me happy."

Liz Rosino ran Columbus, Ohio's Craftin' Outlaws show for years before deciding to leave for grad school in Washington. "I put my heart and soul and sweat and tears into that show for years. It was a difficult decision—it feels like my baby!" It took a while to hand over the reins entirely. "I started the event and covered every detail of the show completely by myself up until last year's event. It was getting so much bigger than I could handle on my own, and I needed to get others interested so it could continue in my absence," she says. "My hope is that it will be more of a committee-run event, and I'll definitely stay on and advise from across the country. Of course, I want to come back and sell as a vendor again, too."

Going Full Time

Maybe you like the craft biz so much that you want to do it full time! This brings a whole new set of challenges, though if you're already running your business in line with IRS requirements, it'll be a lot easier.

Jessica Manack would love to go full time with Miss Chief Productions but feels daunted. "When I think about working for myself, conceptually it appeals to me. But the comfort of having an external employer who pays for good benefits is really appealing," she says. "It's a tricky choice to make when you're getting a good response to your work. You might feel like it's the right time to go full time, but in five years, your style might not be hot anymore."

If you're working with a partner, it's worth it to get legal protections for the both of you so your friendship doesn't go down the tubes if your business does. Here are some other things to think about if you want to take your business to the next level:

- **Incorporation.** Upgrading to this business structure offers more protection and requires the help of a lawyer.

- **Hiring help.** Are you ready to be a manager?

- **Writing a book.** Share your knowledge!

- **Getting on TV.** DIY Network and HGTV have been a boon for crafters.

- **Licensing your work.** You make some cash and give up some creative control.

Epilogue

If I had to boil down this book's business advice to three points, it would be these:

- Be informed.

- Be confident.

- Be yourself.

Crafty Superstar is just a jumping-off point in your pursuit of indie business. I am definitely not a tax wizard or legal guru, so you should follow up with experts (like the ones in the appendix on page 138) and be active in your community—crafters love to give advice.

We're all in this for the love of craft, and our flaws and quirks are what make us—and our products—unique. Have fun with whatever you do. Make your own rules and change them whenever necessary. If you don't really want to build a Martha Stewart-size empire, why put that kind of pressure on yourself? (But if you do become the next Martha, remember your good pal Grace.)

Talking to all these crafters got me hella excited, and I hope you feel the same way. Channel your chutzpah and be the crafty superstar you always dreamed of!

APPENDIX A:
Forms and Templates

Use the templates in this section as a jumping-off point to create your own forms. You can photocopy the forms in this section to use for your business, or you can use them as templates to create your own custom forms.

Price Calculator Template

Use this template, based on Lauren Bacon's pricing philosophy, to get an idea of what you should charge for your goods. Compare your results to similar hand-made items' prices to get an idea of what buyers pay. (Note: If you never, ever intend to sell wholesale, you can use the wholesale price as your retail price.)

A) Cost of materials per item: _____

B) Ideal hourly wage: _____

C) Hourly wage multiplied by the number of hours it takes to make an item: _____

D) Administrative costs per year
(Web site hosting fees, craft show costs, promotional expenses, equipment purchases, etc.): _____

E) Per-hour cost (administrative costs divided by 2,080):

_____

F) Number of hours it takes to make an item multiplied by the per-hour cost: _____

G) Total cost per item (add lines A, C and F): _____

H) Wholesale price (line G multiplied by two): _____

I) Retail price (line H multiplied by two): _____

Invoice Template

Your Company Name
Mailing Address
Phone
E-mail

Date
Invoice No.:

Bill to:

Ship to:

Shipping Method:

Terms:

Quantity	Item	Description	Price	Total for Item

Subtotal:

Tax:

Shipping:

Balance Due:

Inventory Form

Item Name	Description	Cost (wholesale or retail)

Quantity Sold	Buyer Name	Sale Date

Consignment Form

Item Name	Date Out	Quantity

Store	Contact Info	Sales

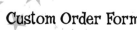

Custom Order Form

Cost Estimate:

Shipping:

Total:

ORDER FORM

Date:

Customer Name:

Mailing Address:

Phone:

E-mail Address:

Description of Items:

Monthly Budget Form

This will help you track your monthly income and expenses, and it includes all the figures you need when filing a 1040-Schedule C. A bookkeeper, or

			Total up to this month	Total this month	Total to date
25	Tax-other				
26	Selling Exp.				
27	Supplies				
28	Telephone				
29	Trade Dues				
30	Traveling Exp.				
31	Wages and Comm.				
32	Water				
34					
35	Sub-total				
51	Non-Deductible				
52	Notes payable				
	Federal Inc. Tax				
53	Loans payable				
54	Loans rec'd.				
55	Personal				
56	Fixed assets				
57					

Total up to this month

Total this month

Total to date 33

Notes:

the Internet, can help explain the headings and determine which expeditures are applicable to you.

Month of:										
	Income		Expenses							
Day	Activity	Amount	Acct. No.	Deductible Accounts	Total up to this month	Total this month	Total to date			
1			1	Materials						
2			2	Accounting						
3			3	Advertising						
4			4	Auto Expense						
5			5	Cartons, etc.						
6			6	Contributions						
7			7	Delivery						
8			8	Electricity						
9			9	Entertainment						
10			10	Freight						
11			11	Heat						
12			12	Insurance						
13			13	Interest						
14			14	Laundry						
15			15	Legal Expense						
16			16	Licenses						
17			17	Misc. Exp.						
18			18	Office exp.						
19			19	Postage						
20			20	Rent						
21										

131

APPENDIX B:
Craft Communities

Online

No matter your craft or your location, you'll find kindred spirits in online craft communities. Some go-getters belong to all of them, but most folks find one or two they really dig and get posting.

Get Crafty
www.getcrafty.com

Craftster
www.craftster.org

Etsy
www.etsy.com

Indiepublic
www.indiepublic.com

MyCraftivity
www.mycraftivity.com

Ravelry
www.ravelry.com

SuperNaturale
www.supernaturale.com

The Switchboards
www.theswitchboards.com

ThreadBanger
forum.threadbanger.com

Offline

Gotta get out of the house? Check out these established crafty communes to see if there's a group near you. If not, start one!

The Church of Craft
www.churchofcraft.org

Craft Mafia
www.craftmafia.com

Stitch 'n Bitch
www.stitchnbitch.org

General Social Networking

Cover all your bases and create a profile, group or fan page for your own brand on all of these popular social networking sites.

Facebook
www.facebook.com

Flickr
www.flickr.com

MySpace
www.myspace.com

Twitter
www.twitter.com

APPENDIX C:
Awesome Crafty Blogs

Check these out for great crafty inspiration. And when you get your own blog set up, trade links and hellos.

Anything Indie

www.anythingindie.com
Andrea highlights the hottest indie designers.

CRAFT

blog.craftzine.com
Projects, shows, inteviews—everything!

Craftsanity

www.craftsanity.com
Podcasts, projects and videos.

Design*Sponge

www.designspongeonline.com
Grace's taste is impeccable, as is her blog.

Etsy's Storque

www.etsy.com/storque
News and trends from Etsy HQ.

Extreme Craft

www.extremecraft.com
Garth finds the weirdest crafts and can't stop writing about them.

Funky Finds

funkyfinds.blogspot.com
Cool stuff from crafters, artists and designers.

Hello Craft

www.hellocraft.com
This DIY nonprofit hosts events and has a killer blog and podcast.

Indie Fixx

www.indiefixx.com
Hot designs and stylish crafts.

Modish

www.modish.typepad.com
Super stylin' handmade highlights.

Naughty Secretary Club

naughtysecretaryclub.blogspot.com
The home of Jennifer Perkins, creator of sassy projects inspired by music, pop culture and vintage goodies.

Plush You

plushyou.blogspot.com
Sweet stuff from Kristen Rask's Seattle shop.

APPENDIX D:
Craft-Friendly Publications

Want to get a project published or promote your business? These magazines are all friends of the craft community. Check their Web sites for submission guidelines.

Bitch Magazine
Landmark feminist magazine
www.bitchmagazine.org
4930 NE 29th Ave.
Portland, OR 97211

BUST
Femininst glossy with star power
www.bust.com
P.O. Box 1016
Cooper Station
New York, NY 10276

CRAFT
Online-only magazine devoted to indie craft
www.craftzine.com
Submissions: www.craftzine.com/cs/user/create/idea

CROQ Zine

DIY craft zine
www.croqzine.com
Submissions: www.croqzine.com/submissions.html

ReadyMade

DIY projects to decorating
www.readymade.com
1716 Locust St.
Des Moines, IA 50309

Venus Zine

Femininst take on pop culture
www.venuszine.com
2000 N. Racine, Suite 3400
Chicago, IL 60614

Vogue Knitting

High-fashion knitting how-to
www.vogueknitting.com
233 Spring St., 3rd Floor
New York, NY 10013

APPENDIX E:
Small Business Resources

Access to Health Insurance/Resources for Care
www.ahirc.org

Business.gov
www.business.gov

Canadian Intellectual Property Office
www.cipo.gc.ca

Design*Sponge's Biz Ladies Events
www.designspongeonline.com/bizladies

Interactive Business Planner
www.canadabusiness.ca/ibp

IRS Resources
www.irs.gov/businesses/small

LawHelp
www.lawhelp.org

NOLO (Law books, legal forms and legal software)
www.nolo.com

SCORE (Counselors to America's Small Business)
www.score.org

U.S. Copyright Office
www.copyright.gov

U.S. Patent and Trademark Office
www.uspto.gov

U.S. Small Business Administration
www.sba.gov

Volunteer Lawyers for the Arts
California: www.calawyersforthearts.org
Canada: www.carfacontario.ca
Colorado: www.lawyersforthearts.org
District of Columbia: www.thewala.org
Georgia: www.glarts.org
Illinois: www.law-arts.org
Indiana: www.indycall.org
Louisiana: www.artscouncilofneworleans.org
Maine: www.mainevla.org
Maryland: www.mdartslaw.org
Massachusetts: www.vlama.org
Michigan: www.artservemichigan.org
Minnesota: www.springboardforthearts.org
Missouri

    Kansas City: www.kcvlaa.org
    St. Louis: www.vlaa.org
New Hampshire: www.nhbca.com/lawyersforarts.php
New Jersey: www.njvla.org
New York: www.vlany.org
North Carolina: www.ncvla.org
Ohio: www.clevelandbar.org
Pennsylvania

    Philadelphia: www.artsandbusinessphila.org/pvla
    Pittsburgh: www.pittsburghartscouncil.org/vla.htm
Rhode Island: www.artslaw.org
Tennessee: www.tnvla.org
Texas: www.talarts.org
Washington: www.thewla.org
Wisconsin: www.artswisconsin.org

Women's Business Enterprise National Council
www.wbenc.org

APPENDIX F:
Reading List

The Anti 9-to-5 Guide: Practical Career Advice for Women Who Think Outside the Cube by Michelle Goodman (2006, Seal Press)

The Boss of You: Everything A Woman Needs to Know to Start, Run, and Maintain Her Own Business by Lauren Bacon and Emira Mears (2008, Seal Press)

Buying In: The Secret Dialogue Between What We Buy and Who We Are by Rob Walker (2008, Random House)

The Crafter Culture Handbook by Amy Spencer (2007, Marion Boyars Publishers)

Guerrilla Marketing series by Jay Conrad Levinson (Houghton Mifflin)

Handmade Nation: The Rise of DIY, Art, Craft and Design by Faythe Levine and Cortney Heimerl (2008, Princeton Architectural Press)

Living the Creative Life: Ideas and Inspiration from Working Artists by Ricë Freeman-Zachery (2007, North Light Books)

The Savvy Crafter's Guide to Success: Turn Your Crafts Into a Career by Sandra McCall (2008, North Light Books)

Small Time Operator: How to Start Your Own Business, Keep Your Books, Pay Your Taxes & Stay Out of Trouble by Bernard Kamoroff (2008, Bell Springs Publishing)

Wear Clean Underwear: Business Wisdom from Mom; Timeless Advice from the Ultimate CEO by Rhonda Abrams (2000, Dell)

APPENDIX G:
Online consignment shops

BuyOlympia.com
www.buyolympia.com

Copacetique
www.copacetique.com

Cut + Paste
www.cutxpaste.com

Little Paper Planes
www.littlepaperplanes.com

Shana Logic
www.shanalogic.com

MY MY
www.mymy.us

APPENDIX H:
Supplies

You know where to find a good supply of yarn, fabric and other crafty materials. But these retailers offer necessary supplies like packaging and marketing materials.

American Science & Surplus

Glass beakers, rolls of magnet tape, bulk raffia and paleo-futuristic calculators? Check.
www.sciplus.com

eBay

An obvious choice for manufactured goods, but supplies are rampant, too.
www.ebay.com

Freecycle

Unload stuff you're not using and pick up other local people's stuff for free. Can't get any cheaper than that.
www.freecycle.org

Hollanders

This Ann Arbor store has every kind of paper you'd ever want; shop online or make a pilgrimage!
www.hollanders.com
410 N. Fourth Ave., Ann Arbor, MI 48104

Hollo's Papercraft

If you're in the Cleveland area, this is a must-see shop. It's packed to the gills with remnants, oddities and every size of envelope you'll ever need. (No online sales.)
www.geocities.com/hollospapercraft
1878 Pearl Road, Brunswick, OH 44212-3252

Moo

Upload your images to make super cute and super stylish mini cards, business cards and more.
www.moo.com

Prints Made Easy

Upload your design to get postcards and business cards quickly and really cheap.
www.printsmadeeasy.com

Sticker Guy!

Making vinyl stickers at low prices for independent businesses since 1993.
www.stickerguy.com

Uline

Amazing assortment of bulk shipping materials.
www.uline.com

APPENDIX I:
Major North American Indie Craft Shows

KEY:

Number of vendors per show
★: under 75
★★: 75–150
★★★: 150+

Vendor fee
$: under $50
$$: $50–150
$$$: $150+

California

Bust Holiday Craftacular
★ $$$
www.bust.com/craftacular
Los Angeles
Annual

Felt Club
★★ $$$
www.feltclub.com
Los Angeles
Annual

Maker Faire/Bazaar Bizarre
★ $$
www.bazaarbizarre.org
San Francisco
Annual

The Renegade Craft Fair
★★ $$$
www.renegadecraft.com
San Francisco
Annual

The Renegade Craft Fair
★★★ $$$
www.renegadecraft.com
Los Angeles
Annual

District of Columbia

**Crafty Bastards!
Arts & Crafts Fair**
★★★ $$
www.washingtoncitypaper.
com/craftybastards
Biannual

Georgia

Indie Craft Experience
★★ $$
www.ice-atlanta.com
Atlanta
Biannual

Kraftwork
★ $
www.ice-atlanta.com
Atlanta
Monthly

Illinois

The DIY Trunk Show
★★ $$
www.diytrunkshow.com
Chicago
Annual

The Renegade Craft Fair
★★★ $$$
www.renegadecraft.com
Chicago
Annual

The Renegade Holiday Sale
★★★ $$$
www.renegadecraft.com
Chicago
Annual

Maryland

Squidfire
★ $$
www.squidfire.com
Baltimore
Biannual

Massachusetts

Bazaar Bizarre
★★★ $$$
www.bazaarbizarre.org
Boston
Annual

Michigan

Detroit Urban Craft Fair
★ $$
www.detroiturbancraftfair.com
Detroit
Annual

Minnesota

Craftstravaganza
★★ $$
www.craftstravaganza.com
St. Paul
Annual

No Coast Craft-o-Rama
★★ $$
www.nocoastcraft.com
Minneapolis
Annual

Missouri

Rock-n-Roll Craft Show
★★ $
www.rocknrollcraftshow.com
St. Louis
Annual

New York

Bust Holiday Craftacular
☆ $$$
www.bust.com/craftacular
New York
Annual

Bust Spring Fling Craftacular
☆ $$$
www.bust.com/craftacular
Brooklyn
Annual

Renegade Craft Fair
☆☆☆ $$$
www.renegadecraft.com
Brooklyn
Annual

North Carolina

The Handmade Market
☆ $$
www.thehandmademarket.com
Raleigh
Biannual

Ohio

Bazaar Bizarre
☆ $$
www.bazaarbizarre.org
Cleveland
Annual

Craftin' Outlaws
☆ $$
craftinoutlaws.luckykat.net
Columbus
Annual

Oklahoma

The Girlie Show
☆ $$$
www.thegirlieshow.net
Oklahoma City
Annual

Oregon

Crafty Wonderland
☆ $$
www.craftywonderland.com
Portland
Monthly

Pennsylvania

Handmade Arcade
☆☆ $$
www.handmadearcade.com
Pittsburgh
Annual

Rhode Island

Craftland
☆☆☆ $
www.craftlandshow.com
Providence
Annual

Texas

Maker Faire/Bazaar Bizarre
☆ $$
www.bazaarbizarre.org
Austin
Annual

Urban Street Bazaar
★ $$$
www.urbanstreetbazaar.com
Dallas
Biannual

Vermont
Queen City Craft Bazaar
★ $
www.queencitycraft.com
Burlington
Annual

Washington
I Heart Rummage
★ $
www.iheartindie.com
Seattle
Monthly

Urban Craft Uprising
★★ $$$
www.urbancraftuprising.com
Seattle
Triannual

Wisconsin
Art vs. Craft
★ $$
Milwaukee
Biannual

Holiday Craftacular
★ $$
www.glitterworkshop.com/
dish/craftacular
Madison
Triannual

Canada
City of Craft
★ $$
www.cityofcraft.com
Toronto, ON
Annual

Got Craft?
★ $$
www.gotcraft.ca
Vancouver, BC
Biannual

I Heart Crafts Bazaar
★ $$
www.iheartcraftsbazaar.
blogspot.com
Vancouver, BC
Quarterly

Contributors

Lauren Bacon

www.laurenandemira.com

Lauren is a veteran Web designer, who co-founded Raised Eyebrow Web Studio, Inc. with her business partner, co-author and all-around right-hand woman, Emira Mears. The two have been in business together for eight years, and during that time have developed a reputation for designing elegant and highly user-friendly Web sites for nonprofit organizations and small businesses.

Grace Bonney

www.designspongeonline.com

Design*Sponge editor Grace Bonney has been a contributing editor at *CRAFT* magazine. The Brooklyn-based writer launched Design*Sponge, a Web site devoted to home and product design, in August 2004. Grace also runs the D*S Biz Lady Series, a national series of meetups for women running design-based businesses, which have been held in Brooklyn, Chicago, Philadelphia, Portland, Seattle, San Francisco, Los Angeles and Boston. Grace hosts and speaks at these events designed to connect local designers and provide free advice on the subjects of PR/marketing, legal concerns, business/financial decisions and wholesaling.

Olivera Bratich

www.whollycraft.net

Olivera is a part-time community health educator and full-time owner of Wholly Craft! in Columbus, Ohio. Her background is in feminist activism and academia, but she couldn't resist the call of craft and entrepreneurship. She's thrilled to be in a position to help support other crafters and build a community of resistance to mass-production. Outside of crafting and "shop talk," her interests include documentary film, gender performance, rabble-rousing and karaoke. She resides in Ohio with her partner and their two beautiful kitty cats. She believes that craft may not save the world, but it can only help.

Jesse Breytenbach

jezzeblog.blogspot.com

Jesse Breytenbach has a master's degree in printmaking and works as a freelance illustrator. In her spare time, she draws comics and recently published a graphic novel. One of her Etsy shops, jezzeprints.etsy.com, is for work on paper, both linocuts and comics. The other shop, jezze.etsy.com, is for handprinted textiles and screenprinted ceramics. She tries out new ideas and documents her works in progress on her blog.

Annie Chau

www.imogene.org

Annie Chau lives and works in Baltimore (known to locals as Charm City) with her boyfriend and two darling and hilarious pit bulls. She grew up in Florida, and studied jewelry and metalsmithing at Towson University in the Baltimore suburbs. After graduating in 2005, she decided to stick around. She's also a proud member of the Charm City Craft Mafia.

Cinnamon Cooper

www.poise.cc

Cinnamon Cooper is a proud Chicagoan, righteous craftivist, and is convinced the revolution will be crafted. As a co-creator of the DIY Trunk Show and a founding member of the Chicago Craft Mafia, she's convinced that her little bit of work has made Chicago a city more accepting of small creative businesses and more interested in handmade quality. Her political and activist interests influenced the direction of her Poise.cc business, and have inspired her more popular bags. She's fortunate to like her day job, but looks forward to the day when her craftivism pays her mortgage.

Susie Ghahremani

www.boygirlparty.com

Susie Ghahremani is a 2002 graduate of the Rhode Island School of Design (RISD) with a BFA in illustration. Her artwork combines her love of nature, animals, music and patterns. Born and raised in Chicago, Susie now happily spends her time painting, drawing, crafting and tending to her pet finches and cat in San Diego, California.

Kati Hanimägi

www.oddballpress.com

Kati Hanimägi launched Oddball Press in July 2007, but was crafting for many years before she encountered her first letterpress. Kati studied printmaking at the Atlanta College of Art and the School of the Art Institute of Chicago before moving to Cleveland. She spends about three-quarters of her time on Oddball stuff and the other quarter as a museum employee.

Jenny Harada

www.jennyharada.com

Jenny Harada's mom taught her how to sew when she was 7 years old, and she's been making stuff ever since. Most of the time she makes wacky stuffed animals, but she likes making all sorts of other things too. She lives in New Jersey with her cute husband, two cute little babies and a cute doggie.

Jenny Hart

www.sublimestitcher.com

Jenny Hart is the founder and creative director of Texas-based embroidery design company Sublime Stitching. Jenny is an internationally published artist and illustrator, and an award-winning author of multiple titles for Chronicle Books. Jenny lives and works in Austin, Texas, where she is a founding member of the infamous Austin Craft Mafia. Despite a hectic schedule, Jenny still finds plenty of time for embroidering.

Taryn Hipp

www.mymy.us

Taryn Hipp is a lady from Doylestown, Pennsylvania. In 2004 Taryn started MY MY, an online shop for handmade awesomeness, after years of making and hoarding items. In June 2007 she opened a retail store under the same name; nine months later she closed the store and started rethinking her goals. Taryn is all about crafting, writing, re-arranging furniture, and is currently organizing a punk rock flea market in Doylestown.

Anne Holman

www.anneholman.com

Anne Holman received her BFA from the Columbus College of Art and Design in Columbus, Ohio. She's currently a full-time studio artist. Her jewelry can be found at boutiques across the country as well as online and at various art festivals and gallery exhibitions throughout the year.

Julianna Holowka

www.meancards.com

Julianna Holowka was born in Detroit, Michigan, to a family of artists and crafters. Always drawing and creating, she went on to earn a degree in industrial design. Chicago was the proving ground where she defined her style—working to create stage productions, album covers, and poster art for various artists and musicians. Julianna now lives in Philadelphia with her fiancé, photographer Chris Crisman, where she designs and constructs a line of homewares and is the principal and creator of Mean Cards for Many Occasions.

Hannah Howard

www.lizziesweet.com

Hannah Howard is an artist based in New York City. She's the creative whirlwind behind Lizzie Sweet, a handmade boutique label inspired by burlesque, pin-up art and the glamour of yesteryear. An avid crafter, her work has appeared in *Stitch and Bitch Nation*, *The Crafter's Handbook* and *Not Another Teen Knitting Book*. She writes about the fabulous side of life and all things crafty at her blog, Superlovelyful (www.superlovelyful.com).

Garth Johnson

www.extremecraft.com

Garth Johnson was born and raised on a farm in Nebraska, attended art school at the University of Nebraska and then got his MFA in ceramics at Alfred University. He's currently a designer at Perkins+Will architects in Atlanta, as well as an adjunct faculty member at Columbus State University in Columbus, Georgia.

Heidi Kenney

www.mypapercrane.com

Heidi Kenney creates happy and sometimes very sad anthropomorphic plush from her home studio in Pennsylvania. She is self-taught and has been running My Paper Crane for almost seven years. The name of her company came from her first attempt at origami, making a paper crane, because she was so amazed that a simple square of paper could be turned into something so beautiful. She has participated in group exhibitions across the globe, including Plush You in Seattle, TINA (This Is Not Art) in Newcastle, Australia, and Plush Week in Los Angeles. Heidi's very first book will be published in 2010.

Holly Klump

www.misshawklet.com

Holly Klump has been a crafter her whole life and has been spinning animal-friendly fibers since misshawklet's birth in 2004. Despite her love of yarn and fibers, Holly is not much of a knitter. Her day job for the past eight years has been working in the library field. She lives in Nashua, New Hampshire, with her man and her pets. In her spare time she plants things.

Faythe Levine

faythelevine.blogspot.com

Seattle-native Faythe Levine has been based in Milwaukee since 2001. She is the founder of Art vs. Craft, an alternative market for handmade goods and was the co-owner of Paper Boat Boutique & Gallery. She is also the director of *Handmade Nation* a feature-length documentary about the rise of DIY art, craft and design as well as the co-author of a book of the same title, published by Princeton Architectural Press in 2008.

Samantha Lopez

www.knotstudio.com

Samantha A. Lopez was born in Mexico City but spent most of her time as a child in the countryside of the state of Morelos. She moved to New York City to study at Pratt Institute of Art and Design, where she received her degree in fine art with a concentration in sculpture. Her work has been exhibited at the Rubelle and Norman Schafler Gallery and Object Image Gallery in Brooklyn. Her book, *Knitted Wire Jewelry: Techniques, Projects, Inspiration* was published by North Light Books in 2009. The Knotstudio line of jewelry can be found online at www.knotstudio.com as well as in select boutiques in the New York City area.

Jessica Manack

www.misschiefshop.com

Her college roommate introduced her to the wonders of button making, and Jessica Manack has never looked back. She's been crafting since 2001 as half of Miss Chief Productions. After trying to sell her wares at ladyfests, flea markets and zine festivals, she was thrilled when a network of indie craft shows suddenly sprung up around the country. Jessica has been on the organizing committee of Pittsburgh's Handmade Arcade since its inception. While she loves living in the Steel City, her hometown, she is always ready to hop in the car, plastic tarps and a stack of singles in tow, to check out the next fair.

Caitlin Phillips

www.rebound-designs.com

Caitlin Phillips has been a book lover since before she could read. As a young child, she devoured books with an intensity matched only by her passion for craft. Inspired by her mother—a quilter, crafter and Girl Scout leader—Caitlin began creating recycled art almost as soon as she could hold scissors. Caitlin's first job after high school was working at the Book Alcove in Gaithersburg, Maryland, and her love for books followed her to Tufts University, where she graduated with a double major in English and drama. In 2004, Rebound Designs was born, and Caitlin began selling her crafty creations full time at the historic Eastern Market in Washington, D.C. Caitlin also exhibits at a variety of shows, from the funky Crafty Bastards in D.C. to the prestigious American Craft Council Show in Baltimore.

Kristen Rask

www.schmancytoys.com

Kristen Rask was born in Cleveland, Ohio. In 1998, she landed in Seattle, which she has made her home. In 2004, she opened a small store in downtown Seattle called Schmancy, where she sells vinyl and plush toys and other crafty goods. Since her opening, she has been invited to curate art shows from New York City to San Francisco. She curates an annual show, Plush You!, at her store (and a few others), which received so much attention that North Light Books published the book *Plush You!* in 2007. She is also the author of *Button and Stitch* (North Light Books, 2009). She is the director of PR and marketing for Urban Craft Uprising and continues to enjoy the art of making stuff as much as she can.

Index

About the Author

Grace Dobush is a magazine editor by day and crafter by night. She and her bookbinding quasi-business, gracie sparkles books (crafty.gracedobush.com), have made appearances at Cleveland's Bazaar Bizarre, Pittsburgh's Handmade Arcade and Renegade Brooklyn. A proud alumna of Kent State's journalism school, Grace has written about craft, art and design for *HOW, Venus Zine* and *The Artist's Magazine*, among others.

Learn more at
www.craftysuperstar.com.

BECOME A CRAFTY SUPERSTAR WITH THESE OTHER NORTH LIGHT BOOKS

Anticraft

Whether you are a crafting outcast, a dark-hearted misfit or just plain tired of mainstream projects, you will swoon over Anticraft. Includes a variety of knitting, crochet, beading and sewing projects from 19 slightly sinister designers with a flair for the unexpected.

ISBN-10: 1-60061-030-7
ISBN-13: 978-1-60061-030-1
Paperback, 160 pages, Z1356

Living the Creative Life

This in-depth guide to creativity is full of ideas and insights from inspiring artists, shedding light on what it takes to make art that you want to share with the world, and simply live a creative life.

ISBN-10: 1-58180-994-8
ISBN-13: 978-1-58180-994-7
Paperback, 144 pages, Z0949

The Savvy Crafter's Guide to Success

Do you want to change crafting from a hobby to a career? Renowned stamp artist Sandy McCall did just that, and she shares the secrets of a successful career in crafts with you!

ISBN-10: 1-58180-942-5
ISBN-13: 978-1-58180-942-8
Paperback, 128 pages, Z0656

These and other fine North Light Books are available at your local craft retailer, bookstore or online supplier, or visit our Web site at www.mycraftivitystore.com.